Also by André Aciman

Letters of Transit: Reflections on Exile and Memory

Out of Egypt: A Memoir

False Papers

False Papers

❊

André Aciman

Farrar • Straus • Giroux

New York

Farrar, Straus and Giroux
19 Union Square West, New York 10003

Copyright © 2000 by André Aciman
All rights reserved
Distributed in Canada by Douglas & McIntyre Ltd.
Printed in the United States of America
Designed by Jonathan D. Lippincott
First edition, 2000

Library of Congress Cataloging-in-Publication Data

Aciman, André.
    False papers / André Aciman.
        p.   cm.
    ISBN 0-374-29978-1 (alk. paper)
    1. Aciman, Andrâ—Journeys—Egypt.   2. Jews, Egyptian—New York
(State)—New York—Travel.   3. Alexandria (Egypt)—Description and travel.
4. Jews—Egypt—Alexandria—Biography.   I. Title.

F128.9.J5 A353 2000
916.2'1—dc21   00-027766

The essays in this collection have appeared in *Commentary, Condé Nast Traveler,
Contentville, The New York Review of Books, The New York Times, The New York
Times Magazine, The New Yorker,* and *The Yale Review.*

For Susan,

my lodestar, my love

Contents

Three Tales

False Papers

Alexandria:

The Capital of Memory

>|<

To those who asked, I said I went back to touch and breathe the past again, to walk in shoes I hadn't worn in years. This, after all, was what everyone said when they returned from Alexandria—the walk down Memory Lane, the visit to the old house, the knocking at doors history had sealed off but might pry open again. The visit to the old temple, the visit to Uncle So-and-so's house, the old school, the old haunts, the smell of the dirty wooden banister on days you almost glided downstairs on your way to a movie. And then, of course, the tears, the final reckoning, the big themes: the return of the native, the romance of the past, the redemption of time. All of it followed by predictable letdowns: the streets always much narrower than before, buildings grown smaller with time, everything in tatters, the city dirty, in ruins. There are no Europeans left, and the Jews are all gone. Alexandria is Egyptian now.

As I step onto the narrow balcony of my room at the Hotel Cecil and try to take in the endless string of evening lights speckling the eastern bay, I am thinking of Lawrence Durrell and of what he might have felt standing in this very same hotel more than fifty years ago, surveying a magical, beguiling city—the "capital of memory," as he called it, with its "five races, five languages . . . and more than five sexes."

That city no longer exists; perhaps it never did. Nor does the Alexandria I knew: the mock-reliquary of bygone splendor and colonial opulence where my grandmother could still walk with an umbrella on sunny days and not realize she looked quite ridiculous, the way everyone in my family must have looked quite ridiculous, being the last European Jews in a city where anti-Western nationalism and anti-Semitism had managed to reduce the Jewish population from at least fifty thousand to twenty-five hundred by 1960 and put us at the very tail end of those whom history shrugs aside when it changes its mind.

The Alexandria I knew, that part-Victorian, half-decayed, vestigial nerve center of the British Empire, exists in memory alone, the way Carthage and Rome and Constantinople exist as vanished cities only—a city where the dominant languages were English and French, though everyone spoke in a medley of many more, because the principal languages were really Greek and Italian, and in my immediate world Ladino (the Spanish of the Jews who fled the Inquisition in the sixteenth century), with broken Arabic holding everything more or less together. The arrogance of the retired banker, the crafty know-it-all airs of the small shopkeeper, the ways of Greeks and of Jews, all of these were not necessarily compatible, but everyone knew who everyone else was, and on Sundays—at the theater, in restaurants, at the beach, or in clubs—chances were you sat next to each other and had a good chat. My grandmother knew Greek well enough to correct native Greeks, she knew every prayer in Latin, and her written French, when she was vexed, would have made the Duc de Saint-Simon quite nervous.

This is the Alexandria I live with every day, the one I've taken with me, written about, and ultimately superimposed on other cities, the way other cities were originally sketched over the Alexandrian landscape when European builders came, in the middle of the nineteenth century, and fashioned a new city modeled after those they already loved. It was this Alexandria I came looking for—knowing I'd never find it. That did not bother me. For I had come not to recover memories, nor even to recognize those I'd disfigured, nor to toy with the thought that I'd ever live here again; I had come to bury the whole thing, to get it out of my system, to forget, to hate even, the way we learn to hate those who wouldn't have us.

I am, it finally occurs to me, doing the most typical thing a Jew could do. I've come back to Egypt the way only Jews yearn to go back to places they couldn't wait to flee. The Jewish rite of passage, as Passover never tells us, is also the passage back to Egypt, not just away from it.

Until the mid-1950s, Jews had done extremely well in Egypt. They had risen to prominence and dominated almost every profession, and they were among the major financiers who brokered Egypt's passage from a European to a national economy, serving as important conduits for foreign investors. Jews managed a significant share of Egypt's stock exchange and owned some of the biggest banks and almost all the department stores; the country boasted the greatest number of Jewish multimillionaires in the Middle East. Jews, though very few in number, held seats in the Egyptian parliament.

These were, for the most part, observant Jews, but in a cosmopolitan city like Alexandria, where overzealous piety was derided and where friendship was almost never based on creed, many of these Jews were quite relaxed when it came to religion, particularly since most of them, educated in Catholic schools, tended to know more about the religions of others than about their own. Seders, I remember, were rushed affairs; no one wanted to inflict Passover on Christians who happened to be visiting and had been induced to stay for dinner.

Following the Israelis' 1948 defeat of the Arabs, anti-Semitism rose sharply in Egypt, and there were some deadly incidents in the wake of the war. Matters became worse after 1956, when Israel joined forces with France and England in a tripartite attack on Egypt after Nasser nationalized the Suez Canal. British and French residents of Alexandria were summarily expelled from Egypt, as were many Jews; everyone had assets, businesses, and properties seized by the state. Aunts and uncles, friends, grandparents, some of whom hadn't been expelled, read the writing on the wall and left within a few years of the 1956 war, abandoning everything they owned. Most settled in Europe, others in America.

Some, like us, simply waited, the way Jews did elsewhere when it was already too late to hope for miracles. We saw the city change and each year watched European shop names come down and be replaced by Egyptian ones, and heard of streets being renamed, until—as is the case now—I didn't know a single one.

The only street whose name hasn't changed is the waterfront road known as the Corniche, al-Corniche, a thick bottleneck mass of tottering loud vehicles emitting overpowering gas fumes.

I try to rest both arms on the balustrade outside my hotel room, as I'd envisioned doing on receiving the glossy brochure with the Cecil's picture. But the small, Moorish/Venetian-style balcony is entirely taken over by a giant compressor unit; it's impossible to maneuver around it. Bird droppings litter the floor.

Two men are speaking in Arabic downstairs. One is telling the other about his very bad foot and his pain at night. The other says it might go away. They don't know how surreal mundane talk can seem to someone who's been away for thirty years.

On the main square facing the hotel stands the ungainly statue of the Egyptian patriot Sa'ad Zaghlul, one leg forward in the manner of ancient Egyptian statues, except that this one wears a fez. I used to pass by here every morning on my way to school by bus.

Beyond Sa'ad Zaghlul is a villa housing the Italian consulate, and farther yet is the city's main tramway station and to its right the Cinema Strand, all unchanged, though worn by age. To my right is Délices, one of the city's best pastry shops. It hasn't moved either. Nothing, I think, is unfamiliar enough. I haven't forgotten enough.

Across the bay sits the fortress of Kait Bey, its ill-lit, brooding halo guarding the Eastern Harbor. The fortress is said to occupy the site of the ancient Pharos lighthouse, one of the Seven Wonders of the Ancient World. Some say that the fort was built with stones taken from the old lighthouse itself. A French archaeological company has been commissioned to dig here. The area is cordoned off and considered top secret.

Not far from the dig lies the Western Harbor, which the ancients used to call the Harbor of Safe Return, Portus Eunostos, from the Ancient Greek *eu*, meaning good, safe, and *nostos*, meaning return. Nostalgia is the ache to return, to come home; *nostophobia*, the fear of returning; *nostomania*, the obsession with going back; *nostography*, writing about return.

So this is Alexandria, I think, before shutting the window, feeling very much like Freud when, in his early forties, he had finally achieved his lifelong dream of visiting Athens and, standing on the Acropolis, felt strangely disappointed, calling his numbness derealization.

I look at my watch. It is one in the afternoon New York time. I pick up the telephone to call America. After a short wait, I hear my father's voice. In the background, I make out a chorus of children, mine probably—or is it the clamor of a school recess down his block?

"How is it?" he asks. I describe the view from my window.

"Yes, but how is it?" he presses. What he means is: has it changed, and am I moved? I can't find the right words.

"It's still the same," I reply. "It's Egypt," I finally say, all else failing.

Each year the city sees many ex-Alexandrians return and wander along its streets. Like revenants and time travelers, some come back from the future, from decades and continents away, A.D. people barging in on B.C. affairs, true anachronoids drifting about the city with no real purpose but to savor a past that, even before arriving, they know they'll neither recapture nor put behind them, but whose spell continues to lure them on these errands in time. The Portuguese have a word: *retornados*, descendants of Portuguese settlers who return to their homeland in Europe centuries after colonizing Africa—except that they are African-born Europeans who return to Africa as tourists, not knowing why they come, or why they need to come again, or why this city that feels like home and which they can almost touch at every bend of the street can be as foreign as those places they've never seen before but studied in travel books.

The first thing I want to do tonight is roam the streets by myself. The downtown shops are still open, and people are literally spilling out into the streets, an endless procession of cars going up the rue Missallah (Obelisk), renamed rue Saffeyah Zaghlul after the patriot's wife. The same stores stand in exactly the same spots, the same pharmacies, bookstores, restaurants; and everywhere the unbroken chain of shoe stores and third-tier haberdasheries with wares dangling over the sidewalks, and always that muted spill of lights which reminds me of Cavafy's nights and Baudelaire's Paris. I manage to recognize the Gothic-Venetian window sashes of an old restaurant. When I walk into Flückiger's, the pastry shop, and tell the cashier that I am just looking around, she smiles and says, as she must have done to hundreds like me, "*Ah, vous êtes de nos temps,*" as if time could ever belong to anyone. Do I want to buy cakes? I shake my head. "They're still the same. We're still Flückiger," she adds. I nod. One would have thought that I shopped there every day and had stopped now on my way from work, only to change my mind at the last minute. The idea of eating cake to summon my past seems too uncanny and ridiculous. I smile to myself and walk out through the beaded curtain. It hasn't changed either. Nor have the buildings. They are far more beautiful than I remember, the architecture a mix of turn of the century French and floral Italian. But they are also grimier, some of them so run-down it's impossible to tell how long they've got. It's no different with cars here. Many are rickety thirty-plus patched-up jobs, part rust, part tin, part foil; soldered and painted over with the sort of Egyptian ingenuity that knows how to preserve the old and squeeze residual life out of objects which should have perished long ago but whose replacement will neither come from abroad nor be manufactured locally. These are not really cars but, rather, elaborate collages of prostheses.

I turn right and walk into a murky street that used to be called rue Fuad. Next to the Amir Cinema looms a strange, large structure I have never seen before. It is the newly dug-up Roman amphitheater I've been reading about. I ignore it completely and turn left, where I spot Durrell's pastry shop, and walk down a narrow street, where I find the Cinema Royale and, right across from it, the old Mohammed Ali, now known as the Sayyed Darwish Theater, the pride of Alexandria's theater elite.

And then it hits me. The Mohammed Ali is my last stop tonight; I now have nowhere else to turn but the Hotel Cecil. To my complete amazement, I have revisited most of my haunts in Alexandria in the space of about eight minutes!

Once on the crowded streets again, I walk the way I have come, along the edge of the sidewalk, my eyes avoiding everyone else's, my gait hurried and determined, everything about me trying to discourage contact with a city that is, after all, the only one I think I love. Like characters in Homer, I want to be wrapped in a cloud and remain invisible, not realizing that, like all revenants, I am perhaps a ghost, a specter already.

The next morning, I head out on another exploratory walk. But in fifteen minutes I have already reached Chatby, the very place I was meaning to see last. This is where most of the cemeteries are located. Perhaps I should pay a visit to my grandfather's tomb now.

I try to find the Jewish cemetery, but am unable to. Instead, I head in a different direction and decide to visit my great-grandmother's house. As soon as I near her neighborhood, I find myself almost thrust into the old marketplace. It, too, hasn't changed since my childhood. The pushcarts and open shops are still in place, as is the unforgettable stench of fish and meat, and always the screaming and the masses of people thronging between stacks of food and crates of live chickens.

I could go upstairs, I think, once I reach the building on rue Thèbes, but people are watching me fiddle with my camera, and someone actually pops his head out of the window and stares. I decide to leave. Then, having walked to the next block, I change my mind and come back again, trying to let the building come into view gradually, so as to hold that magical moment when remembrance becomes recovery. I am resolved not to be intimidated this time and make my way straight to the main doorway.

A woman appears with a child in her arms; she is the caretaker's wife; the caretaker died a few years ago; she is the caretaker now. A man also shows up. He lives on the street floor, he says in English, and has lived there since the early fifties. I tell him I, too, lived here once, at number 15. He thinks for a moment, then says he doesn't remember who lives there now. I tell the caretaker that I want to knock at apartment 15. She smiles and looks at me with suspicion. She is thinking. "Sit Vivi," she says, Mme Vivi. I am almost on the verge of shaking. Vivi was my great-aunt. "They left," she says. Of course they left, I want to shout, we all left thirty years ago! "May I knock at the door?" I ask. "You may," she replies, with the same smile, "but no one is there." When will they be back? She looks at me with a blank stare. No one has occupied the apartment since.

I know that if I push the matter and tip her well, I might persuade her to show me the apartment. But the thought of a dark apartment where no one's been for three decades frightens me. Who knows what I'd find creeping about the floor, or crawling on the walls. It's all well and good for a German to go digging for the ghost of Troy or sifting through Helen's jewels. But no Trojan ever went back to Troy.

When I point to the elevator and ask her whether *it* still works, she laughs. *It* had died long ago. And she adds, with inimitable

Egyptian humor, *"Allah yerhamu."* May God have mercy on its soul.

I step into the main courtyard and look up to our old service entrance: I can almost hear our cook screaming at the maid, my mother screaming at the cook, and the poor maid's heartrending yelp each time the tumor on her liver pressed against her spine. I am trying to decide whether I should insist and ask to be taken upstairs, or perhaps she could show me another apartment in the same line. I see a cat playing in the foyer; next to it is a dead mouse. The caretaker does not notice it. Even the man from the first floor doesn't seem to notice, doesn't care.

I know I'll regret not insisting, and also that this is typical of my perfunctory, weak-willed attempts at adventure. But I am tired of these ruins, and the smell of the old wood panels in the foyer is overpowering. Besides, this is how I always travel: not so as to experience anything at the time of my tour, but to plot the itinerary of a possible return trip. This, it occurs to me, is also how I live.

Outside, I spot an old woman with a shopping basket; she looks European. I ask her whether she speaks French. She says she does. She is Greek. I am almost ready to tell her about my entire life, everything about my grandparents, my mother, our apartment that has never been lived in since the day we left so many years ago, and all these ruins scattered everywhere, but I break in mid-sentence, hail a cab, and ask to be taken to the museum—by way of the Corniche, because I want to see the water.

The Corniche always breaks the spell of monotonous city life, the first and last thing one remembers here. It is what I think of whenever I sight a beckoning patch of blue at the end of a cross street elsewhere in the world. The sky is clear and the sea is stunning, and my cabdriver, who speaks English, tells me how much he loves the city.

The Graeco-Roman Museum was where I would come to be alone on Sunday mornings in 1965, my last year in Alexandria.

I pay the fee and, as usual, rush through the corridors and the quiet garden, where a group of Hungarian tourists are eating potato chips. The Tanagra statuettes, the busts of Jupiter and of Alexander, the reclining statue of a dying Cleopatra, all these I pass in haste. There is only one thing I want to see, a Fayoum portrait of a mummified Christian. I linger in the old, musty room. The painting is exquisite indeed, more so than I remember. But I am astonished that this bearded man looks so young. There was a time when he was older than I. Now I could almost be his father. Otherwise, nothing has changed: I'm standing here, and he's lying there, and it's all as if nothing has happened between one Sunday and the next.

I want to buy his picture in the museum shop. There are no postcards of Fayoum portraits. I want to buy E. M. Forster's guide to the city, but they haven't had it in a long time. I ask whether they have any of the Durrell books. They haven't carried those in a long time either. There is, in fact, really very little to buy. And very little else to see. I have seen everything I wanted to see in Alexandria. I could easily leave now.

An entire childhood revisited in a flash. I am a terrible nostographer. Instead of experiencing returns, I rush through them like a tourist on a one-day bus tour. Tomorrow I must try to find the cemetery again.

Outside the museum, I am reminded of my grammar school nearby. I remember coming here in high school hoping to pay a quick visit to my old school and getting lost instead. I know I've strayed into the once-affluent Greek neighborhood. But I also know that I'm lost exactly where I lost my way thirty years earlier. The thought amuses me. I used to come here for private English lessons twice a week. I remembered the teacher, and her sumptuous home, and the luxurious china in which I, at the age of seven, would have to drink tea. I remember a poem by Wordsworth, the dim-lit living room with many flowers and perfumes, and my father coming to pick me up after tutorial, discussing books with her. I would sit and listen, and watch them talk, as other guests kept arriving.

I thought I recognized her building and decided, why not, Mademoiselle Nader might still be there. I look at the names on the mailboxes, but there is no Nader. I see the name *Monsieur et Madame E. Nahas* and assume they are Syrian-Lebanese. Perhaps they might tell me where she lives. As I am ascending the stairs, I happen upon a name on a brass plate; it's the name of a very old school friend. I ring his bell. The Filipino maid speaks good English; I explain I used to know her employer. He is in Europe, she replies. She shows me into a living room streaming in daylight. I sit on the sofa and scribble a note for him, leaning over to the tea table. Then I hand it to her and ask whether she knows of a certain Mademoiselle Nader. Never heard of her. I say goodbye and continue climbing the stairs until I've reached the Nahas residence. They're not home either, and their maid has never heard of the Naders. A delivery boy, who happens to be coming up the stairs, seems to remember something and asks me to knock at another apartment. An old woman, speaking impeccable French, says that of course she remembers Marcelle Nader, whom she calls Lola. Lola died two years ago, totally alone, impoverished, and broken-spirited. Her family had lost everything during the mass nationalizations of 1961. She and her sister would rent out rooms in their large home, but even then, that hardly constituted an income. When her sister left for Switzerland, Lola was forced to give private lessons to businessmen who, it seems, had other things in mind but who settled for English the more she aged. In the end, she sold her apartment to, of all people, my old school friend downstairs. I hadn't recognized the apartment at all. Perhaps it was on the same sofa and at the same tea table that I'd learned English.

Turb'al Yahud, Alexandria's Jewish cemetery, is located at the opposite end of the Armenian cemetery and lies only a few steps away from the Greek Orthodox. Farther down the quiet, dusty, tree-lined road is the Catholic cemetery. Magdi, a native Alexandrian who is employed by the American school I attended as a child, swears that Turb'al Yahud must be somewhere close by but can't remember where. "I come here only once a year—for my mother," he explains, pointing to the Coptic cemetery not far along the same road.

Magdi double-parks and says he will ask directions from the warden of the Armenian cemetery. We have been driving around for more than two hours in search of my parents' old summer beachside home, but here, too, without luck. Either it's been razed or it lies buried in a chaos of concrete high-rises and avenues built on what used to be vast stretches of desert sand. Soon Magdi comes out, looking perplexed. There are, as it turns out, not one but two Jewish cemeteries in the area.

"Which one has a gate on the left?" I say, remembering my very early childhood visits to my grandfather's grave four decades ago.

"That's the problem," says Magdi, drawing on his cigarette. "Both have gates to the right."

I am dismayed. I can situate the grave only in relation to the left gate. We decide to try the nearest cemetery.

Magdi starts the car, waits awhile, then immediately speeds ahead, leaving a cloud of dust behind us. In a matter of minutes we have parked on a sidewalk and ambled up to a metal gate that looks locked. Magdi does not knock; he pounds. I hear a bark, and after a series of squeaks, a man in his early fifties appears at the door. I try to explain in broken Arabic the reason for my visit, but Magdi interrupts and takes over, saying I have come to see my grandfather's grave. The warden is at a loss. Do I know where the grave is? he asks. I say no. Do I know the name, then?

I say a name, but it means nothing to him. I try to explain about the gate to the left, but my words are getting all jumbled together. All I seem to remember is a pebbled alleyway that started at the left gate and crossed the breadth of the cemetery.

The warden has a three-year-old son wearing a very faded red sweatshirt bearing the initials CCCP—not unusual in a place where ancient relics come in handy. Their dog, fleeced from the neck down, has a large bleeding ulcer on his back.

"Oh, *that* gate," the warden responds when I point to another, much smaller gate at the opposite end of the cemetery. "It's locked, it's never been used." Indeed, the gate at the end of the alleyway looks welded in place. I am almost too nervous to hope. But I pick my way to the end of the path and, having reached the area near the left gate, climb over a wild bush whose dried leaves stick to my trousers, turning with a sense of certainty that I am trying to distrust, fearing the worst.

"Is this it?" asks Magdi.

I am reluctant to answer, still doubting that this could be the spot, or this the marble slab, which feels as warm and smooth to the touch as I knew it would each time I rehearsed this moment over the years. Even the name looks dubious.

"Yes," I say, pointing to the letters, which I realize Magdi can't read.

The warden knows I am pleased. His son trails behind him. A fly is crawling around his nose. Both of them, as well as the warden's wife, are barefoot, Bedouin style.

I take out my camera. Everyone is staring at me, including the warden's ten-year-old daughter, who has come to see for herself. It turns out that no Jew ever visits here. "No one?" I ask. "*Walla wahid*," answers the daughter emphatically. Not one.

There are, it occurs to me, far more dead Jews in this city than there will ever again be living ones. This reminds me of what I saw in a box at the main temple earlier this morning: more skullcaps than Jews to wear them in all of Egypt.

The warden asks whether I would like to wash the tombstone. I know Magdi has to go back to work; he is a bus driver and school ends soon. I shake my head.

"Why?" asks the warden. "*Lazem.*" You must.

I have lived my entire life outside rituals. Now I am being asked to observe one that seems so overplayed and so foreign to me that I almost want to laugh, especially since I feel I'm about to perform it for them, not for me. Even Magdi sides with the warden. "*Lazem,*" he echoes.

I am thinking of another ritual, dating back to those days when my father and I would come on quiet early-morning visits to the cemetery. It was a simple ritual. We would stand before my grandfather's grave and talk; then my father would say he wished to be alone awhile and, when he was finished, hoist me up and help me kiss the marble. One day, without reason, I refused to kiss the stone. He didn't insist, but I knew he was hurt.

I pay the warden's family no heed and continue to take pictures, not because I really want to, but because in looking through the viewfinder and pretending to take forever to focus, I can forget the commotion around me, stand still, stop time, stare into the distance, and think of my childhood, and of being here, and of my grandfather, whom I hardly knew and scarcely remember and seldom think of.

I am almost on the point of forgetting those present when the warden appears, lugging a huge tin drum filled with water. He hoists it on a shoulder and then splashes the dried slab, flooding the whole area, wetting my clothes, Magdi's, and the little boy's feet, allowing the stone to glisten for the first time in who knows how many decades. With eager palms, we all go about the motions of wiping the slab clean. I like the ritual. Magdi helps out silently, but I want it to be my job. I don't want it to end. I am even pleased that my clothes are wet and dirty.

I still can't believe I was able to find my grandfather's grave so quickly. Memories are supposed to distort, to lie. I am at once comforted and bewildered.

In the distance I can hear the tireless drone of Alexandria's traffic, and farther off the loud clank of metal wheels along the tramway lines—not obtrusive sounds, for they emphasize the silence more—and I am reminded of how far Grandfather is from all this: from all these engines; from the twentieth century; from history; from exile, exodus, and now return; from the nights we spent huddled together in the living room, knowing the end had come; from our years in cities he had never visited, let alone thought some of us might one day call home. Time for him had stopped in the early fifties on this dry, quiet, secluded patch of dust that could turn into desert in no time.

I look around and recognize famous Jewish names on tombstones and mausoleums. They, too, like my grandfather, were lucky not to have seen the end. But they also paid a price: no one ever comes here. The opulent mausoleums, built in Victorian rococo, were meant to house unborn generations that have since grown up elsewhere and don't know the first thing about Egypt.

"Are you happy now?" I want to ask my grandfather, rubbing the stone some more, remembering a tradition practiced among Muslims of tapping one's finger ever so gently on a tombstone to tell the dead that their loved ones are present, that they miss them and think of them. I want to speak to him, to say something, if only in a whisper. But I am too embarrassed. Perhaps this is why people say prayers instead. But I don't know any prayers. All I know is that I cannot take him with me—but I don't want to leave him here. What is he doing here anyway? In a hundred years, no one will even know my grandfather had lived or died, here or elsewhere. It's the difference between death and extinction.

I pretend to want to take another picture and ask Magdi, the warden, and his family to pose in front of one of the palm trees, hoping they will stay there after the picture and leave me alone awhile. I can feel my throat tighten, and I want to hide the tears welling up inside me, and I am, once again, glad to cover my eyes with the viewfinder. The warden's daughter comes closer. She wants a picture by herself. I smile and say something about her pretty eyes. I give her father a good tip.

Everyone thinks it's been a good visit. Perhaps all cemetery visits are.

On my last evening in Alexandria, I and a group of young teachers from the American school have gathered at a pizzeria to celebrate someone's birthday. We've parked on a narrow alleyway, halfway on the sidewalk, exactly where my father would park his car. Everyone at the party orders pizza, salad, and beer. It occurs to me that we might easily be in Cambridge or New Haven.

By eleven the party breaks up. Before getting into the car, we take a stroll toward the Church of St. Saba. The streets are very dark, and after spending time in the American bar, I am suddenly confronted with the uncanny thought that we are, after all, very much in Egypt still. Maybe it's the alcohol, but I don't know whether I'm back in Egypt or have never left, or whether this is all a very cruel prank and we're simply stranded in some old neighborhood in lower Manhattan. This, I realize, is what happens when one finally comes home: one hardly notices, and it doesn't feel odd at all.

Later that night, as I'm looking out from my balcony, I think of the young man from Fayoum, and of the young man of fourteen I used to be back then, and of myself now, and of the person I might have been had I stayed here thirty years ago. I think of the strange life I'd have led, of the wife I would have, and of my other children. Where would I be living? I suppose in my great-grandmother's apartment—it would have fallen to me. And I think of this imaginary self who never strayed or did the things I probably regret having done but would have done anyway and don't wish to disown; a self who never left Egypt or ever lost ground and who, on nights such as these, still dreams of the world abroad and of faraway America, the way I, over the years, have longed for life right here whenever I find I don't fit anywhere else.

I wonder if this other self would understand about him and me, and being here and now and on the other bank as well—the other life, the one that we never live but conjure up when the one we have is perhaps not the one we want.

This, at least, has never changed, I think, my mind drifting to my father years ago, when we would stop the car and walk along the Corniche at night, thinking of the worst that surely lay ahead, each trying to give up this city and the life that came with it in the way he knew how. This is what I was doing now as well, thinking of the years ahead when I would look back to this very evening and remember how, standing on the cluttered balcony at the Cecil, I had hoped finally to let go of this city, knowing all the while that the longing would start again soon enough, that one never washes anything away, and that this marooned and spectral city, which is no longer home for me and which Durrell once called "a shabby little seaport built upon a sand reef," would eventually find newer, ever more beguiling ways to remind me that here is where my mind always turns, that here, to quote this century's most famous Alexandrian poet, Constantine Cavafy, I'll always end up, even if I never come back:

> For you won't find a new country,
> won't find a new shore,
> the city will always pursue you,
> and no ship will ever take you away from yourself.

And then I remembered. With all the tension in the cemetery that afternoon, I had forgotten to ask Magdi to show me Cavafy's home. Worse yet, I had forgotten to kiss my grandfather's grave. Maybe next time.

In Search of Blue

❖

Years ago, when I lived in Rome with my mother and brother, and my father was away in France, come Christmas and Easter, and sometimes twice in the summer, we would fill a couple of suitcases and, as though the whole thing had been an improvised whim, would call for a cab, find the 3:30 *direttissimo* at Stazione Termini, take out the tickets I had purchased the day before on my way home from school—I was the only one who spoke decent enough Italian to buy tickets—and, before we had time to sit and visualize the entire happy stretch of our trip, were off, as if by magic, to Paris.

Of course, I never thought about the trip beforehand; I pretended to let it be sprung on me. Going to Paris seemed such a farfetched, dreamed-up luxury—an act of hubris almost, considering how poor we were after leaving Alexandria—that it was more out of superstition than thrift that, in an effort not to jinx the trip by assuming it would indeed happen, we invariably found ourselves refusing to buy small presents for those whom we had purposely failed to warn to come meet us at the station.

The trip itself was quite an ugly affair and lasted eighteen hours. The train originated in Naples and was filled with rowdy furloughed soldiers, mothers of immigrants visiting their children in the north with all manner of roped boxes, and middle-aged secretaries who were unfailingly preyed upon by the soldiers. By the time you were awakened at the border, usually at one in the morning, and heard what you thought were the first wisps of French, you were at once overjoyed and in total misery. You were in France! But in the stuffy second-class compartment—where six, sometimes more, had been sleeping with their shoes off—you might as well have been in a barn.

On that train ride, however, there were two magic moments, and I knew them both extremely well. One came toward dawn, when through the steamy windows you felt the train speed along the silent fields of Chambéry, where the fog rose between the trees, blanketing the landscape like white tempera. As far as I was concerned, this was the heartland of the wonderful, beguiling continent called Europe. The other was far more special. It came about two hours, perhaps more, into the trip from Rome, when our train began to elbow the Tuscan and Ligurian coast, racing past large mansions and castles and unending stretches of cypress trees, all of them overlooking what seemed to be the most placid coast in the world. Every other moment, however, these splendid vistas were interrupted by a tunnel, an old wall, or by houses built too close to the tracks, frustrating my desire to savor these villas and views long enough to imagine I inhabited them. And yet that is how I learned to worship the Tyrrhenian and Ligurian Seas: in abrupt slices, in thwarted splendor, as if the whole thing were unreal and untenable—the way the trip to Paris had to remain unreal and untenable for it to happen.

I never bothered to stare long enough at the names of the stations along the coast, and the sea always came unannounced. Part of the magic lay in not knowing exactly when it would come, or whether it would come at all, or whether, not being as beautiful as I thought it was, it had come and gone without my knowing.

For years this wonderful expanse of still and timeless blue, where hills and rippleless beaches seemed made to exist in memory alone, belonged nowhere. I never saw pictures of it, never heard anyone mention it; it simply retreated into a hinterland of tiny places with strange names: Viareggio, Forte dei Marmi, La Spezia, Cinque Terre, Rapallo. I came across some of the names while reading about the lives of Byron, Shelley, and Stendhal. But that was all.

Yet this twenty-minute view, interrupted and obstructed as it was, remained the most beautiful thing I had ever seen. What made it so spellbinding might have been leaving Italy, which I disliked in those days, or the joy of going to Paris, where everyone said we would eventually move. Or perhaps it was simply the once-familiar, ordinary pleasure—now a luxury—of having a prolonged view, however imperfect, of the sea. For an Alexandrian, used to having the beach within sight all day long, it was like meeting a close sibling two years after a quarrel: an odd mix of strained familiarity, sudden intimacy, and wistful reminders that, despite embraces, things might never be the same.

Not that I hadn't seen the beach in Italy before. But this was different. This had timelessness, magnitude, spirituality—not the attraction of an exalted swimming pool, which was what the beaches of Rome held for me. This was the beach year-round: beach as a way of life, beach at hand's reach, beach in the blood. Just as in Alexandria. Passing by so extended a seascape was like passing by Alexandria, the way we do in dreams, waving hello to a house that is no longer ours, that belongs to others but might revert to us any moment now, because the universe would make so much sense if it indeed did. It made me remember beach life more keenly, made me long for it, made me know exactly what I could almost touch, and lacked, and might cry for. That, after all, was why it was so beautiful—because it was familiar, because I had finally found it again, because I had become a stranger to it, because it was made to be lost. Losing the sea was already embedded in every image of the sea. You look at it because it isn't, and could never be, really there; because it wasn't yours, and would never be yours again.

What broke the spell—or rather, what magnified it—was the fact that during a brief trip I took fifteen years later, a girl and I, armed with Eurailpasses, having sped by this selfsame spot and having decided that this was perhaps the most perfect place in the world, suddenly got off the train a few stations later, at Nervi. Neither of us had heard of the town. We didn't have hotel reservations. It was ten o'clock at night. And it was raining. But we did not feel that the situation could turn against us. We asked a cabdriver to take us to the best hotel, assuming that such a hotel would offer the most spectacular view of the sea, all the while fearing that the rooms would be taken. When we arrived, I got out of the cab, told the driver not to turn off his engine—a propitiatory gesture—and rushed in to ask what I expected to be a perfunctory question about vacancies. The answer surprised me. Yes, they did have rooms. With a view? Naturally, *signore*. Balcony as well? How else? Ten minutes later we were sitting on a balcony overlooking the poorly lit cliffs of Nervi and Bogliasco, watching the raging waves crash against the rocks at night, as in any Romantic poem.

The next morning, when we awoke and opened the French windows, I found what I feared I would never find again in my life.

Let me correct myself: I found what I feared I would find but could never afford to hope I might find and, indeed, continue to hope I'll never find again—because I wouldn't know what to do with it, because losing the sea makes living in New York easier to accept, because I want to take the sea on my terms, not on hers, because I want it all or nothing, knowing full well that ultimatums with people, much less with the sea, are intentionally unacceptable.

What I found that morning was perfect swimming weather, perfect blue sea, perfect blue sky, perfect breakfast delivered to our perfect little room and consumed on the most perfect little table on the most perfect balcony. After swimming, it was back to the balcony. After lunch, back to the balcony. After a long nap, back to the balcony. Not much time for sightseeing. There was nothing to see in Nervi. I took out my diary and, feeling quite inspired, could write only the following terribly humbling words:

E di tutto questo mare, cosa faccio?

It is impossible to translate what these words mean. First, because I'm not so sure they mean anything in proper Italian. But let me attempt to render them thus: "And what am I to do with all this water?" It was an expression of helplessness before overwhelming bounty. It's what you say when you've been given a huge, unwieldy present that you're unable (or reluctant) to accept—a carton of books, a huge box of chocolates, or even a second life, complete with childhood and adolescence all over again. Or it's like having a huge dessert heaped on your plate as you think to yourself with greed and gratitude and no few misgivings: Am I really expected to finish all of this? Wouldn't you like to take some back? I am not used to so much. Must I eat it all now? Can I take some home? How do I live this down? Can't you make it go away?

It almost sounded as if I had been . . . inconvenienced. Instead of being enthralled by the sight, instead of expressing great joy at finally being in this very spot which years earlier had reminded me of an Alexandria-done-better, the words that came to me were almost a lament, a whine. I might as well have been complaining. I was so used to deferral and denial that when confronted with plenitude, I caught myself wishing it had never existed.

Perhaps my seeming nonchalance or disappointment came from something too frontal, too invasive, too munificent in the spectacle. I wanted it more diluted, more fragmented, oblique, obstructed—as it had been on my train rides to Paris so many years earlier—even though it was precisely this fragmented nature of the vista that I used to find so irksome and frustrating. Sitting on my balcony, I kept staring at the fabulous expanse of blue, and all I could think of, besides feeling helpless, was: *There it is. I'm leaving in three days!* I wanted to close my eyes. I was in the most perfect spot on earth. There was, now that I think of it, nothing more to want. Nothing more to say.

But that was the problem. There was nothing to write about, nothing to invoke—nothing was happening. Everything I knew how to do proved, on this occasion, quite useless. There was, to use a current term, no narrative.

Thinking—as any bookish man is always reminded when confronted by the hard-and-fast business of life, of the body, of pleasure—comes after, not before, and certainly not during. To the question "What am I to do with all this water?" the answer should have been "Swim."

Never in my life had I been served such a huge dish and been left feeling so hungry, so worried. Like a rich immigrant who comes back to his little native town hoping to impress the locals but finds that if he fails to recognize them, they couldn't care less that he hasn't, I didn't even know what to feel, much less what I felt, except for this admixture of numbness and joy. I finally decided to publish these words in a memoir: "All this sky and all this water—what do you do with so much blue once you've seen it?" The words were not so much a question as a statement of despair, of defeat, of profound irony. It was just a question—to which I knew there was no answer.

What do you do with so much blue once you've seen it? meant: I cannot touch any of it—just look and be glad I saw. But can one just stand and stare and leave things alone that way?

What do you do with so much blue once you've seen it? meant: How do I take this stunning expanse back to America? And why, why be so tempted now that I've made my peace with America? Isn't it pointless to be given this blue, which I love so much but which I've grown to love if for no other reason than because I've allowed myself to think it could exist only in memory and is therefore unreal?

What do you do with so much blue once you've seen it? came almost as a reproach, as though I were misexperiencing the sea in the same way, as an adolescent in Egypt, I never wanted to go to the beach for fear of running into those I was dying to meet and pretended to avoid and hoped they'd ask me why.

What do you do with so much blue once you've seen it? What is it if not the desire to prod some kind of admission from those we cannot have and wish we hadn't met or gotten to love and are condemned to crave.

What do you do with so much blue once you've seen it? It's what you ask instead of doing, as if words could provide anything over and above raw experience.

My love of the sea is in part a result of having lost Alexandria, not necessarily something I experienced in Alexandria. I love it precisely because it was lost. The smell of salt, the touch of sunlight on bare skin, and above all the magic of beach life, with its strange, elaborate rituals.

One might as well ask: When, in fact, did I learn to worship the sea?

When, for instance, did I learn to decipher those imperceptible signals by which, while you're still in bed with your eyes closed, you're already able to determine whether there's a white flag, or a red flag, or no flag at all along the beaches?

When did I discover the magic sensation of walking toward the beach without being able to spot the beach yet, and, like all born Alexandrians and seasoned beachgoers who are superstitious, when did I learn to look the other way, if only to pretend I didn't know I was in fact headed to this one place that gives me so much pleasure?

When did I discover the mild anxiety, the *légère angoisse*, of walking toward the beach and catching myself feeling something which, many years later, I realized—probably with the feeling that I might not have overcome it as an adult—was a sense of apprehension and dismay caused by the image of girls upon the beaches, desirable and disturbing, on whose bodies still hovers my fear of desiring, or of desiring too much, or of being snubbed for desiring?

Where did I learn to love the beach at seven o'clock in the morning, or just before noontime, or immediately after lunch, or late in the afternoon, when after swimming for the second time that day one takes a shower and is then greeted by the cool, crisp feel of a clean-scented cotton shirt? Or the pleasure of drying in the sun and hearing friends' voices drifting in and out of what must surely have been, although one keeps swearing it wasn't, a short, unintended nap? There were days when, taking finals in late spring, I would look out the window and suddenly know that this day had beach weather written all over it, that I could almost touch the blueness, although the beaches were nowhere within sight or hearing.

Drop me in Nice or in Anzio or in East Hampton as someone's guest and early on Sunday morning I will look for any excuse to go out to buy the paper and take the long way, not because I need to read the paper or because I need to be alone, but because I want to take time out and think that I am going on a very familiar errand, that I know exactly what I'm doing, and that any moment now I'll end up pushing open a very old gate whose squeak I can't forget. As long as I keep expecting to arrive there and never really hurry back, I will, if I try hard enough, make out the voices of people who have long since died but have suddenly come back and are beginning to complain that I've been gone too long and have almost missed breakfast.

If I long for the sea or for Alexandria, it is because, with the sea around me, I can begin to rebuild my life, put things back together again, pick up where I believe I left off. I collate little snippets of the past, the way those who've been deported map out every corner of their city, their street, their temple.

I look for the sea everywhere, because the sea was the backdrop for almost all the scenes of my childhood. I look for my childhood, for my own gaze looking out at the sea. What I want is not to swim but to have the pleasure of "finding the sea," of guessing and spying the sea, of suggesting the sea, the way children today play at "finding Waldo"—because in finding the sea I find myself.

Anyone who was born on the Mediterranean—and I'm thinking

not so much of beach resorts as of water cities such as Algiers, Marseilles, Naples, Trieste, Istanbul, Beirut, Alexandria—has an internal compass that immediately detects the presence of water nearby: *thalassotropism.* You turn to water. You're alerted neither by smell nor by sounds but by an intense silence, the kind that sits heavily before a late-afternoon snowstorm in other cities—a hollow, airy, unobtrusive silence in which loud noises are instantly muffled by what could only be the quiet sea. Even when you're in a big city, your senses immediately warn you that if you thread your way through the narrowest streets, you'll eventually be led to this dazzling expanse of turquoise and aquamarine.

If I pretend not to notice the sea when I approach it, it is not simply to intensify the pleasure by wedging endless interruptions and intrusions along the way. I go looking for snatches, swatches of blue, not vistas, because people who've lived in water cities see the sea every day but seldom focus their entire attention on it. It is by ignoring the sea, or by re-creating the nonchalance with which I used to ignore the sea, that the sea comes alive for me today. Even my reluctance to go for a swim twice on the same day now becomes the surest reminder of my love for the sea.

It is when I am almost blinded by light in New York City that I remember the sea on glary sunny days. It is by not looking, which is what one did in Alexandria, that I can give myself the surest impression that the sea might just as easily be waiting across the street. I do not look because I do not want to find that I am wrong. I do not look because I am trying to bring about what I am cautious not to claim I want.

That, in the end, is how I love the sea. I love it from across the street. I need distance, obstacles between me and what I want. I like bits and pieces of the beach—even symbols, signs, tokens, totems, fetishes of the beach—the way I like the promise of Paris more than Paris itself, a staggered view more than huge vistas.

I need all these dilatory measures the way Matisse needed them when he painted in Nice. There are almost no paintings with the word "sea" in the works Matisse did in Nice between 1916 and 1930, especially those done at the Hôtel Méditerranée et de la Côte d'Azur. *Interior with a Violin Case, Interior with a Black Notebook, Woman with a Green Parasol on a Balcony, Woman with a Pink Parasol on a Balcony, Pascal's Pensées, The Closed Window*: most show a room leading to another room, which leads to yet another, until you reach a faraway window. Some of these paintings, however, depict a room that leads directly to French windows opening onto a balcony, in between the balusters of which finally appear what lies—for me—at the very core of these paintings: incidental patches of blue, caught almost inadvertently or as an afterthought by the painter, who seems to have merely dabbed a few strokes of paint between each post. Advertisers have seen through the trick: airlines, travel agencies, department stores, and manufacturers of cigarettes, perfume, lingerie, soaps, suntan lotion— all have reinvented the magic resonance of that blue space caught between curved balusters.

Sometimes in Matisse you do not see the balcony or the banister. Instead, the shutters are closed and the room is quite dark. Even so, the slats in the shutters cannot quite belie the explosion of noon light downstairs on the Promenade des Anglais. In the darkened interior of *The Hindu Pose*, for example, behind a bare-chested woman, the most exiguous crack in between the shutters immediately betrays the intensity of summer light in Nice. It may seem that the opened violin case, or the woman with a pink umbrella, or the black mirror placed behind a bowl of sea anemones reflecting a side view of the painter's bed is the true subject of Matisse's eye: in fact, his subject was always the sea. But staggered, deferred, delayed, distanced, recessed, almost serving as a vague background hastily sketched around a precisely executed balustrade and allegedly having no other purpose than to add color to what would have been a stifling scene in a room.

Of course, when I look at these paintings, especially those of 1919, and that room I seem to know as well as my own, I am looking at them as a lover of lost beaches looks at someone else's love of sea color. I want to go to that room because I want to see the place from which Matisse did the one thing every artist is interested in doing with the sea: not to describe it, not even to evoke it, but to invoke it. I want to see the room in which he purposely cultivated the distance between himself and the sea, distracting his gaze, throwing all kinds of objects upon his field of vision as though they were hurdles, placing other rooms and all manner of draperies between his easel and the sea, because now I, too, want to do the same with the sea, the way scholars put a footnote between their subject matter and their love for it. I will visit his hotel bedroom one day, throw open the window shutters the way hotel personnel do after depositing your bags, and staring out to the sea, rather than watch my thoughts drift onto this vast expanse of blue, I will remember that this is a visit to the French window from which Matisse himself might have said, "What do you do with so much blue once you've seen it?" And as I stand there trying to perform the solemn act called "taking it all in," thinking of Nice and the years that have passed between 1919 and 1999, and the sea that allows me to look out into the deep and imagine the vaguest outline of the Eastern Harbor of Alexandria farther out, I know that I will catch myself thinking of the black violin case with the balusters and the ray of light sweeping the floor of Matisse's bedroom. Except that I won't be thinking of this room in Nice but of a picture of it on West Fifty-third Street in Manhattan, at the Museum of Modern Art. I will need this new detour, this new obstacle between me and the sea. Except that the obstacle will now be the painting itself.

Monet must have known this, too. There are scenes of Bordighera, where, standing on top of a hill, Monet would paint a rather gnarled, detailed, scrawny set of pine trees with surrounding foliage; but I suspect that it is the restrained spread of blue in between and above the busy foliage that truly matters, the background that is truly the foreground—the light from the sea, the light-because-of-the-sea that Monet wanted and that Proust so beautifully rendered as the "sun beaming on the sea." The tree stands before us, and downhill lies the town of Bordighera. In fact, from his visit to Bordighera, it seems that Monet painted only one direct seafront, *The Marina in Bordighera*, a rather uninteresting painting. Otherwise, he seems to have avoided all direct contact with the sea. What Monet left us, instead, are collections of scenes of Bordighera: the Moreno gardens, for example, with their lush palm trees, the tufted growth granting but the most meager peek at this distant, immaterial blue—your eyes forced to reach out and find the sea, the way Proust's *plante grimpante* seeks out its object of desire. Sometimes there isn't even a hint of water. Monet, who had written to his wife about "water, beautiful blue water," abstained from painting any water whatsoever. Waterless seascapes.

When you look at *The Villas of Bordighera, Strada Romana in Bordighera, The Valley of Sasso, Grove of Olive Trees in the Moreno Garden, Impressions of Morning, Under the Lemon Trees, Small Country Farm at Bordighera,* and *Palm Trees at Bordighera,* if you have the least *thalassotropic* instinct, you'll immediately intuit, as if all of them were being intentionally coy with you, the indelible presence of the sea. What Monet has done is allow the viewer to suspect that if he peeked in between these villas, or through the foliage in the villa of Mr. Moreno, or turned left or right along the Roman Road—as though he himself were out on a Sunday errand to buy a paper or fresh milk—he would, without fail, perhaps without meaning to or showing much interest, be met by a breathtaking, stunning vista of the sea, where, to quote Aeschylus, the "ocean dropped waveless and windless to his noonday bed."

All this may explain why I was so disappointed when I did go back to Egypt. Early one afternoon I was given a car and a driver. I asked him to take me to where I remembered our beach house was located. We couldn't find the beach house. Instead, as we drove by the coast road, passing the spot where for ten years, almost forty years ago, I had spent every one of my summer days, I felt the usual disappointment one feels on what are supposed to be momentous occasions. Could this really be the beach I had so yearned for on those train rides back and forth between Paris and Rome?

The beach was totally empty and unusually clean on this warm late-October afternoon. After school, we used to come and swim awhile here before heading home to do our homework. Another person might have rushed to the shore and had himself a good swim and gotten the whole thing out of his system. I tried, once again, to take the sea in—with my eyes, with my breath, seeking out words when all else failed. But this was not a Joycean "day of dappled seaborne clouds." Nothing came in. I was, in fact, doing the most normal thing in the world: I was not experiencing anything. Instead, I was comparing. Comparing this beach with the one in Italy, with another in East Hampton, with the one I had dreamed of finding that day a few years ago when I strolled into MoMA and, looking at Matisse, allowed my mind to drift to Alexandria, thinking to myself that, now that I was in Alexandria, perhaps the time had indeed come for me to ask, however diffidently, a question that always humbles me and always comes back to me: *What do you do with so much blue once you've seen it?*

Shadow Cities

※

On a late-spring morning in New York City four years ago, while walking on Broadway, I suddenly noticed that something terrible had happened to Straus Park. The small park, located just where Broadway intersects West End Avenue on West 106th Street, was being fenced off. A group of workers, wearing orange reflector shins, were manning all kinds of equipment, and next to what must have been some sort of portable comfort station was a large electrical generator. Straus Park was being dismantled, demolished.

Not that Straus Park was such a wonderful place to begin with. Its wooden benches were dirty, rotting, and perennially littered with pigeon droppings. You'd think twice before sitting, and if you did sit, you'd want to leave immediately. Also, it had become a favorite hangout for the homeless, the drunk, and the drug-addicted. Over the years the old cobblestone pavement had turned into an undulating terrain of dents and bulges, mostly cracked, with missing pieces sporadically replaced by tar or cement, the whole thing blanketed by a deep, drab, dirty gray. Finally, the emptied basin of what used to be a fountain had turned into something resembling a septic sandbox. Unlike the fountains of Rome, this one, like the park itself, was a down-and-out affair. Never a drop flowed from it. The fountain had been turned off decades ago.

Straus Park was, like so many tiny, grubby parks one hardly ever notices on the Lower East Side, a relic of a past that wasn't ancient enough to have its blemishes forgiven or to feel nostalgic about. One could say the same of the Art Nouveau–style statue of what I took to be a reclining Greek nymph lost in silent contemplation, looking inward, as it were, to avoid looking at what was around her. She looked very innocent, very Old World, and very out of place, almost pleading to be rescued from this ugly shrub that dubbed itself a park. In fact, the statue wasn't even there that day. She had disappeared, sold no doubt.

The thing I liked most about the square was gone, the way so many other things are gone today from around Straus Park: the Olympia Restaurant, the Blue Rose, the Ideal Restaurant, Mr. Kay's Barbershop, the Pomander Bookshop, the Siam Spice Rack, Chelsea Two, and the old Olympia Theater, drawn and quartered, as all the theaters are these days, plus the liquor store that moved across the street but really disappeared when it changed owners, the flower store that went high tech, and La Rosita, which went from down-and-out to up-and-coming.

Why should anybody care? And why should I, a foreigner, of all people, care? This wasn't even my city. Yet I had come here, an exile from Alexandria, doing what all exiles do on impulse, which is to look for their homeland abroad, to bridge the things here to things there, to rewrite the present so as not to write off the past. I wanted to rescue things everywhere, as though by restoring them here I might restore them elsewhere as well. Seeing one Greek restaurant disappear or an old Italian cobbler's turn into a bodega, I was once again reminded that something was being taken away from the city and, therefore, from me—that even if I don't disappear from a place, places disappear from me.

I wanted everything to remain the same. Because this, too, is typical of people who have lost everything, including their roots or their ability to grow new ones. They may be mobile, scattered, nomadic, dislodged, but in their jittery state of transience they are thoroughly stationary. It is precisely because you have no roots that you don't budge, that you fear change, that you'll build on anything, rather than look for land. An exile is not just someone who has lost his home; he is someone who can't find another, who can't think of another. Some no longer even know what home means. They reinvent the concept with what they've got, the way we reinvent love with what's left of it each time. Some people bring exile with them the way they bring it upon themselves wherever they go.

I hate it when stores change names, the way I hate any change of season, not because I like winter more than spring, or because I like old store X better than new store Y, but because, like all foreigners who settle here and who always have the sense that their time warp is not perfectly aligned to the city's, and that they've docked, as it were, a few minutes ahead or a few minutes behind earth time, any change reminds me of how imperfectly I've connected to it. It reminds me of the thing I fear most: that my feet are never quite solidly on the ground, but also that the soil under me is equally weak, that the graft didn't take. In the disappearance of small things, I read the tokens of my own dislocation, of my own transiency. An exile reads change the way he reads time, memory, self, love, fear, beauty: in the key of loss.

I remembered that on summer days many years earlier, when I was doing research on my dissertation, I would sometimes leave the gloomy stacks of Butler Library at Columbia and walk out into the sun down to 106th Street, where I'd find a secluded shaded bench away from the drunks and sit there awhile, eat a sandwich, a pizza, occasionally smiling at some of the elderly ladies who sat, not in the park, but along the benches outside, the way they did on Saturday afternoons around Verdi Square on Seventy-second Street and had probably learned to do on sunny, windy summer days in Central Europe, and as they still do in those mock-English spots in Paris that the French call *petits squares*, where people chat while their children play. Some of these ladies spoke with thick accents. I pictured their homes to myself: lots of lace, many doilies, Old World silverware, mannered Austro-Hungarian everything, down to the old gramophone, the black-and-white pictures on the wall, and de rigueur schnapps and slivovitz.

They made me think of 1950s pictures of New York, where it seems to grow darker much sooner in the evening than it does nowadays, where everyone wears long gray overcoats because winters were always colder then, and when the Upper West Side teemed with people who had come from Europe before the war and then stayed on, building small, cluttered lives, turning this neighborhood into a reliquary of Frankfurt-am-Main—their Frankfurt-away-from-home, Frankfurt-on-the-Hudson, as the old joke goes, but not an inappropriate name for a city which, in Germany today, dubs itself Mainhattan, and which is, ironically enough, a far stranger city to them, now that it imitates Manhattan, than their adopted Manhattan imitating old Frankfurt. There I met old Mrs. Danziger with the tattoo on her arm. Eighty-three-year-old Kurt Appelbaum, a concert pianist in his day, was sitting on such a bench; we spoke; we became friendly; one night, without my asking, he offered to play the *Waldstein Sonata* and the *Rhapsody in Blue* for me. "But do not tape," he said, perhaps because he wished I would, and now that I think of it, I wish I had, as I sat and listened on a broken chair he said had been given to him by Hannah Arendt, who had inherited it from an old German colleague at the New School who had since died as well.

That was the year I rediscovered the Busch Quartet's 1930s recordings of Beethoven, and I imagined its members playing everywhere in those Old World, prewar living rooms around Straus Park. And by force of visualizing them there, I had projected them onto the park as well, so that its benches and the statue and the surrounding buildings and stores were, like holy men, stigmatized by Beethoven's music as it was played by a group of exiles from Hitler's Reich.

I would come every noon, for the statue mostly, because she was, like me, willing to stand by in this halfway station called Straus Park. She reminded me of those statues one finds everywhere in Rome, springing on you from their niches when you least expect them in the evening.

It is difficult to explain what seclusion means when you find it on an island in the middle of Broadway, amid the roar of midday traffic. What I was looking for, and had indeed found quite by accident, was something that reminded me of an oasis—in the metaphorical sense, since this was a "dry" fountain—but an oasis of the soul, a place where, for no apparent reason, people stop on their various journeys elsewhere. Straus Park, it seemed, was created precisely for this, for contemplation, for restoration—in both its meanings—for retrospection, for finding oneself, for finding the center of things.

And indeed there was something physically central about Straus Park. This, after all, was where Broadway and West End Avenue intersected, and the park seemed almost like a raised hub on West 106th Street, leading to Riverside Park on one side and to Central Park on the other. Straus Park was not on one street but at the intersection of four. Suddenly, before I knew why, I felt quite at home. I was in one place that had at least four addresses.

Here you could come, sit, and let your mind drift in four different directions: Broadway, which so far uptown had an unspecified Northern European cast; West End Avenue, decidedly Londonish; 107th Street, very quiet, very narrow, tucked away around the corner, reminded me of those deceptively humble alleys where one finds stately homes along the canals of Amsterdam. And 106th, as it descended toward Central Park, looked like the main alley of a small town on the Italian Riviera, where, after much trundling in the blinding light at noon as you take in the stagnant odor of fuel from the train station where you just got off, you finally approach a cove, which you can't make out yet but which you know is there, hidden behind a thick row of Mediterranean pines, over which, if you really strain your eyes, you'll catch sight of the tops of striped beach umbrellas jutting beyond the trees, and beyond these, if you could just take a few steps closer, the sudden, spectacular blue of the sea.

To the west of Straus Park, however, the slice of Riverside and 106th had acquired a character that was strikingly Parisian, and with the fresh breeze which seemed to swell and subside all afternoon long, you sensed that behind the trees of Riverside Park, serene and silent, flowed an elusive Seine, and beyond it, past the bridges that were to take you across, though you couldn't see any of it yet, was not the Hudson, not New Jersey, but the Left Bank— not the end of Manhattan, but the beginning of a whole bustling city awaiting beyond the trees, as it did so many decades ago, when as a boy in Alexandria, dreaming of Paris, I would go to the window, look out at the sea at night, and think that this was not North Africa at all but the Ile de la Cité. Perhaps what lay beyond the trees was not the end of Manhattan, or even Paris, but the beginnings of another, unknown city, the real city, the one that always beckons, the one we invent each time and may never see, and fear we've begun to forget.

There were moments when, despite the buses and the trucks and the noise of kids with boom boxes, the traffic light would change and everything come to a standstill, and people weren't speaking, and the unrelenting sun beat strong on the pavement, and then one could almost swear this was an early-summer afternoon in Italy, and that if I really thought about it, what lay behind Riverside Park was not just an imaginary Seine but perhaps the Tiber as well. What made me think of Rome was that everything here reminded me of the kind of place all tourists know so well: that tiny empty piazza with a little fountain where, thirsty and tired with too much walking all day, you douse your face, then unbuckle your sandals, sit on the scalding marble edge of a Baroque fountain, and simply let your feet rest awhile in what is always exquisitely clear non-drinkable water.

Depending on where I sat, or on which corner I moved to within the park, I could be in any of four or five countries and never for a second be in the one I couldn't avoid hearing, seeing, and smelling. This, I think, is when I started to love, if "love" is the word for it, New York. I would return to Straus Park every day, because returning was itself now part of the ritual of remembering the shadow cities hidden there—so that I, who had put myself there, the way squatters put themselves somewhere and start to build on nothing, with nothing, would return for no reason other than perhaps to run into my own footprints. This became my habit, and ultimately my habitat. Sometimes finding that you are lost where you were lost last year can be oddly reassuring, almost familiar. You may never find yourself; but you do remember looking for yourself. That, too, can be reassuring, comforting.

On a hot summer day I came looking for water in a place where no water exists, the way dowsers do when they search for trapped, underground places, seeking out the ghost of water, its remanence. But the kind of water I was really looking for was not fountain water at all, Roman or otherwise. I remembered my disappointment in Rome years ago when, dunking my feet in the turtle fountain early one afternoon, it occurred to me that these surreptitious footbaths in the middle of an emptied Rome in August and all this yearning for sunlight, heat, and water amounted to nothing more than a poor man's simulated swim at the beaches of my childhood, where water was indeed plentiful, and where all your body could bathe, not just your toes.

At Straus Park, I had discovered the memory of water. Here I would come to remember not so much the beauty of the past as the beauty of remembering, realizing that just because we love to look back doesn't mean we love the things we look back on.

There is a large fountain in Rome at Piazza Navona, where the four great rivers of the world are represented: the Ganges, the Nile, the Plate, and the Danube. I knew it well, because it stood not far from a small bookstore where, years ago, as a teenager, I would go to purchase one Penguin book a week—a small, muggy,

and sultry shop, of which I recall the sense of bliss on first coming
out into the sun with a new book in my hand. As I surveyed these
four rivers, the question was which do I splash my face in?

There is no frigate like a book, says Emily Dickinson. There is
nothing I have loved more than to take a good book and sit somewhere in a quiet open spot in Rome with so many old things around
me, open up to any page, and begin traveling back sometimes, as
when I read Lawrence Durrell and Cavafy, thinking of time, of all
that retrospection—to quote Whitman—or eagerly looked forward
to the New World, as when I learned to love Eliot and Pound. Does
a place become one's home because this is where one read the
greatest number of books about other places? Can I yearn for
Rome when I am finally standing where I longed to stand when I
was once a young man in Rome?

All this, if it hadn't already, begins to acquire absurd propor-
tions when I realize that, during that dissertation summer of many
years ago, I had applied for and gotten a job to teach in an American high school in Rome. So that as I sat there in Straus Park, going
through my usual pickup sticks and cat's cradles of memories, I had
discovered something rather unique: I didn't want to go to Rome,
not for a year, not for half a year, not even for a month, because it
finally dawned on me that I didn't very much like Rome, nor did I
really want to be in France, or Egypt for that matter—and though I
certainly did not like New York any better, I rather enjoyed my
Straus Park–Italy and my Straus Park–Paris much more, the way
sometimes I like postcards and travel books better than the places
they remind me of, art books better than paintings, recordings better than live performances, and fantasies more than the people I
fantasize about—some of whom are not only destined to disappoint
but can't even be forgiven for standing in the way of the pictures

we originally had of them. Once in Rome, I would most certainly long to be in Straus Park remembering the Rome where I'd once remembered the beaches of my childhood. Italy was just my way of grafting myself to New York.

I could never understand or appreciate New York unless I could make it the mirror—call it the mnemonic correlative—of other cities I've known or imagined. No Mediterranean can look at a sunset in Manhattan and not think of another sunset thousands of miles away. No Mediterranean can stand looking at the tiny lights speckling the New Jersey cliffs at night and not remember a galaxy of little fishing boats that go out to sea at night, dotting the water with their tiny lights till dawn, when they come back to shore. But it is not New Jersey I see when I watch the sunset from Riverside Drive.

The real New York I never see either. I see only the New York that either sits in for other places or helps me summon them up. New York is the stand-in, the ersatz of all the things I can remember and cannot have, and may not even want, much less love, but continue to look for, because finding parallels can be more compelling than finding a home, because without parallels, there can't be a home, even if in the end it is the comparing that we like, not the objects we compare. Outside of comparing, we cannot feel. One may falsify New York to make it more habitable; but by making it more habitable in that way, one also makes certain it remains a falsehood, a figment.

New York is my home precisely because it is a place from which I can begin to be elsewhere—an analogue city, a surrogate city, a shadow city that allows me to naturalize and neutralize this terrifying, devastating, unlivable megalopolis by letting me think it is something else, somewhere else, that it is indeed far smaller, quainter than I feared, the way certain cities on the Mediterranean are forever small and quaint, with just about the right number of places where people can go, sit, and, like Narcissus leaning over a pool of water, find themselves at every bend, every store window, every sculptured forefront. Straus Park allowed me to place more than one film over the entire city of New York, the way certain guidebooks of Rome do. For each photograph of an ancient ruin there is a series of colored transparencies. When you place the transparency over the picture of a ruin, the missing or fallen parts suddenly reappear, showing you how the Forum and the Colosseum must have looked in their heyday, or how Rome looked in the Middle Ages, and in the late Renaissance, and so on. But when you lift all the plastic sheets, all you see are today's ruins.

I didn't want to see the real New York. I'd go backward in time and uncover an older New York, as though New York, like so many cities on the Mediterranean, had an ancient side that was less menacing, that was not so difficult to restore, that had more past than present, and that corresponded to the old-fashioned world I think I come from. Hence, my obsession with things that are old and defunct and that seep through, like ancient cobblestones and buried rails from under renewed coats of asphalt and tar Sealed-off ancient firehouses, ancient stables turned into garages, ghost buildings awaiting demolition, old movie theaters converted into Baptist churches, old marketplaces that are now lost, subway stops that are ghost stations today—these are the ruins I dream of restoring, if only to date the whole world back a bit to my time, the way Herr Appelbaum and Frau Danziger belonged to my time. Going to Straus Park was like traveling elsewhere in time. As Emily Dickinson writes, How frugal is the chariot that bears a human soul!

How uncannily appropriate, therefore, to find out fifteen years later that the statue that helped me step back in time was not that of a nymph but of Memory herself. In Greek, her name is Mnemosyne, Zeus' mistress, mother of the Muses. I had, without knowing it, been coming to the right place after all. This is why I was so disturbed by the imminent demolition of the park: my house of memories would become a ghost park. If part of the city goes, part of us dies as well.

Of course, I had panicked too soon. Straus Park was marvelously restored. After spending more than a year in a foundry, a resurrected statue of Memory remembered her appointed place in the park and resumed her old position. Her fountain is the joy of children and of all the people who lean over to splash their faces on a warm summer day. I go there very often, sometimes to have coffee in the morning after dropping my children off at school. I have now forgotten what the old Straus Park looked like. I do not miss it, but somehow part of me is locked there, too, so that I come here sometimes to remember my summer of many years ago as well, though I am glad those days are gone.

My repeated returns to Straus Park make of New York not only the shadow city of so many other cities I've known but a shadow city of itself, reminding me of an earlier New York in my own life, and before that of a New York which existed before I was born and which has nothing to do with me but which I need to see—in old photographs, for example—because, as an exile without a past, I like to peek at others' foundations to imagine what mine might look like had I been born here, where mine might be if I were to build here. I like to know that Straus Park was once called Schuyler Square, and before that it was known as Bloomingdale Square, and that these are places where everything about me and the city claims a long, continuous, call it a common, ancestral, imaginary past, where nothing ever bolts into sudden being, but where nothing ever disappears, not those I love today, nor those I've loved in the past, that

Old World people like Herr Appelbaum, who played Gershwin for me on 105th Street one night when he could have played Schubert instead, and Mrs. Danziger, who never escaped the Nazis but brought them with her in her dreams at night, might still sit side by side with Ida Straus, who refused to board the lifeboats when the *Titanic* sank, and stayed on with her husband—that all these people and all these layers upon layers of histories, warmed-over memories, and overdrawn fantasies should forever go into letting my Straus Park, with its Parisian Frankfurts and Roman Londons, remain forever a tiny, artificial speck on the map of the world that is my center of gravity, from which radiates every road I've traveled, and to which I always long to return when I am away.

But perhaps I should spell the mystery out and say what lies at the bottom of all this. Straus Park, this crossroad of the world, this capital of memory, this place where the four fountains of the world and the four quarters within me meet one another is not Paris, is not Rome, could not be London or Amsterdam, Frankfurt or New York. It is, of course, Alexandria.

I come to Straus Park to remember Alexandria, albeit an unreal Alexandria, an Alexandria that does not exist, that I've invented or learned to cultivate in Rome as in Paris, so that in the end the Paris and the Rome I retrieve here are really the shadow of the shadow of Alexandria, versions of Alexandria, the remanence of Alexandria, infusing Straus Park itself now, reminding me of something that is not just elsewhere but that is perhaps more in me than it ever was out there, that it is, after all, perhaps just me, a me that is no less a figment of time than this city is a figment of space.

Square Lamartine

-›|‹-

My romance with Paris begins, as one says of earthquakes, at an epicenter—surrounded by tall, turn-of-the-century buildings, a small empty park, and silent avenues. This is how I always pictured Paris as an adolescent, before ever seeing it. A *marchand de tabacs* who would sell me cigarettes without asking questions; a *pâpeterie* where I could buy a longed-for Pelikan pen; the smile of girls outside a vaguely imagined lycée; a secret rendezvous at the cinema.

Before I had ever set foot there, France was already my homeland, the place to which I knew I would eventually return. But everything stood in my way, starting with the fact that in the early 1960s, roughly the time of which I am speaking, my family was still living in Alexandria, decades away from 1960s Paris. There were other inconvenient circumstances as well: many adult members of my family, although educated as French-speakers in the schools of the Alliance Israélite Universelle, had somehow managed to become not French but Italian citizens. Then, too, I myself had gone to English schools throughout my childhood and hence knew

English better than French—so that, if my mother tongue was French, I still spoke it with a strange accent. (This was part of my problem all around; I spoke several languages with a French accent, except French.)

Here I was, a Jewish boy landlocked in Nasser's anti-Semitic Egypt, yearning to be back in a France I had never seen and did not even belong to. As we were losing our fortune, and the Egyptian police closed in on us with house inspections, harassing phone calls at night, anonymous letters, secret denunciations, what could be better than to sit at the window in my great-aunt's bedroom at night and imagine myself staring at the Seine—which, she never tired of telling me when she joined me and glued her forehead to the windowpane, flowed ever so close to her old apartment in Paris? "Can you actually see the Seine from your windows?" I would ask. "No, but it's scarcely seven minutes away." And then she would recite the refrain of Guillaume Apollinaire's poem "*Le pont Mirabeau*":

> *Vienne la nuit sonne l'heure*
> *Les jours s'en vont je demeure*

> Let night fall and the hours go by
> The days pass on, still I stay

It was of those "scarcely seven minutes away" that I kept thinking during my last months in Egypt as we sold what we could and packed the rest, amid daily squabbles between my mother and her mother-in-law and an aunt who could not help taking sides and always picked the wrong one. I learned to understand in the course of those days that there are places on the planet we simply must accept that we shall never see again. I thought this place was Egypt. Little did I know that, as with men who repeatedly lose women for the same reason, there are families who lose their homes at least once every generation.

I remember exactly the French authors, old and new, I was reading back then: Molière, François Mauriac, Alain-Fournier, Jean Anouilh, Georges Duhamel, Albert Camus. Like the window in my aunt's bedroom, they looked out onto what seemed the most distantly adjacent spot on earth. All I needed to do was read a sufficient number of pages and I could almost be there, in André Gide's Paris or Marcel Pagnol's Marseilles, the imagined sound of France blending with the perpetual shouting in Arabic that rose up to my room from the street below.

There was another book that appeared from nowhere one day, mixed in among the volumes my father had dumped in a pile in the packing room, a book I assumed he had no need of but later understood he must have left around in the manner of parents who want their sons to know certain things before they find out about them from more direct and less desirable sources. I devoured it, it devoured me. Each sentence opened up a world so vast and so thrilling that at the end of each night's perusal I wished I could forget everything I had just read so as to discover it afresh the next morning. "You will find," I read on one of the pages, "that, when you're about fourteen or older, should you happen to be walking about at night, certain overdressed women may come up to you and ask you to accompany them. It is better that you do not."

I was fourteen. But who were these women, and why had none ever approached me? And why was I not already in France, where overdressed women came up from under the cover of night and asked you to accompany them? I looked out the window at my imagined Seine with its imagined bridges and quais that stood seven minutes away from our imagined new home. But this was not Paris; it was still Alexandria.

During our last days in Egypt I learned to my shock that our destination was not to be my imagined Paris but some down-to-earth, working-class neighborhood in Rome. Thus we ended up— my mother, my brother, and I, for my father remained behind for the time being in Egypt—in Italy. We knew no one, barely spoke the language, and did not know where to shop, or how. At night, feeling totally hemmed in by this country we could not love or fathom, we would close the shutters to stave it off. But Italy would not go away: from the buildings surrounding our courtyard there came each evening the echo of an entire society tuned to the same television channel. Sometimes the noise arose from a nearby movie theater, which, on warm summer nights, opened its roof to allow us to hear the roar of laughter or the dubbed voice of Sean Connery. When school started that fall, our twilit street turned sordid, with its grimy groceries, the coffee merchant whose dark quarters looked more like a cave than a shop, the corner bar filling up with workers stopping for wine on the way home from work. How could this be my home?

Then came a miracle. My father, who after leaving Egypt had found a temporary job in France, summoned us for a two-week visit during the winter holiday break, *pour voir*, just to see. He made our visit seem a mere stopover, Paris on consignment, on spec. More than three decades later, I can still remember what we did on each and every one of those fifteen days.

I remember my first visit to the Latin Quarter, where I went with my older girl cousins and their fiancés, all undergraduates and all, apparently, Parisians. On a rainy weekday afternoon we whizzed through narrow streets crowded into two tiny Citroën *deux chevaux* to catch a Humphrey Bogart revival. One of us jumped out to purchase tickets, another to find snacks, while the rest looked for parking places. After the movie we stopped at a café, where everyone ordered tea.

Another day, on our way to buy cigarettes for everyone, my cousin took me into a record shop. She was looking for Bach's double-violin concerto. Sitting in a tiny booth, we stole a few minutes to listen to the recording with David Oistrakh as the principal soloist. She found it not to her liking. Did they have Menuhin? They did not. We went across the street, where they had neither Oistrakh nor Menuhin but they did have Heifetz—the best, according to the salesgirl. No, thanks. For the next two weeks, we listened to violinist after violinist. To this day the sound of the double concerto brings to mind those heady first encounters with Paris, when I watched for signs of snow that never came and fell in love with the cool grayness that settled over the city at teatime, presaging evenings when we would crowd into the car and tour Paris-by-night, invariably ending our adventure with crêpes, onion soup, and Vichy candies.

Was it Paris or just the stuffed car and the good fellowship of cousins I had not seen in at least a decade that made me feel I was here to stay? The streets bustling with people my age who spoke my language; the spirited jokes; the movie theaters filled to capacity—this was not just the center of the world, or even the center of my life, it was me. It was my voice, if not when I spoke, then something clearer and deeper, as when I laughed.

Perhaps it was not even a voice but a manner of being in the world that made me love that world and, come to think of it, myself as well.

When after about four days we finally visited my great-aunt in the 16th arrondissement, it was like walking into our old home in Alexandria—smaller, to be sure, but the exact same kind of home: the same feel, the same smell, the same familial injunctions to be quiet and mind our manners. But this apartment was like a finished version of the rough sketch that had been our home in Alexandria. If Egypt was the bass melody, Paris was the full orchestral score, an entire city beaming with the glory of a redeemed déjà vu. Like Saint Augustine thinking back to the time when he had not yet loved God, only to wonder why he could not have known Him sooner, I, too, asked: Why wasn't I born here, why can't I live here, when will it happen, why am I here when it seems too late?

My father had said these two weeks were to be a tryout. But preliminaries were totally unnecessary. I was ready to settle in at a moment's notice.

One night, in a tiny park not far from my great-aunt's, my father pointed out two girls in their mid-teens: "I'll bet you anything they live in the neighborhood; they probably go to the Lycée Janson de Sailly." Immediately, I wanted to be in school.

I was too young to know how to seize any opportunities that might come my way. But presentiments of romance were everywhere. From the way women looked at me, I could tell that this was a language whose syntax I already knew fluently; all I needed was the vocabulary. And then, of course, there were those over-dressed women who under cover of night would surely come up and ask me to accompany them. They were the reason I could not wait for the chance to be on my own in Paris—no easy task, since so many relatives were hosting us. But my great-aunt finally gave me my opening. In her refrigerator she liked to keep bottles of water taken from the Lamartine fountain down the block, an artesian well whose water Jacques Hillairet, in his *Dictionnaire Historique des rues de Paris*, had described as having *"un goût fade"* (an insipid taste). She assigned me the job of keeping them filled.

Never has anyone managed to turn so simple an errand into so time-consuming a task. There were always people at Square Lamartine, including others my age probably doing the same thing as I for their grandparents or parents. Wedged among them as I waited my turn at the fountain, I became not only a real Parisian but a young Jacob, waiting to meet his Rachel at the well of Beersheba. Next time, I thought, as, day after day, I failed to muster the courage to speak.

I came every day, sometimes twice, sitting on a bench and reading when the weather was not too cold, dawdling to watch the sunset and the last girls leave before dragging home the heavy bottles stuffed into two plastic net bags. Over tea one evening, my aunt said she was convinced I was smoking, while my grandmother opined that I was just slow and my mother that I must be losing my place to aggressive housewives. As for my father, he credited me with cunning schemes I let him think were successful.

When, by early January, it became clear that we had to return to Rome, I felt I would die before I could board the train. It was leaving on a Saturday evening, and would arrive in Rome on Sunday afternoon; on Monday we would be back in school. All I could think of on my last day at Lamartine was that Sunday evening in Rome—opening our suitcases, putting everything back in its dull place in an apartment from whose shuttered windows indelible sounds would make it impossible to imagine we were still in Paris, even though our suitcases would still smell of Paris, and the sound of Bach would remind me of Paris, as would the cheap pens with the sliding Eiffel Tower I was planning to buy before leaving, or the punched metro ticket, and the residual pack of Vichy candies stuffed inadvertently into my coat pocket to be recovered weeks into our humdrum Roman lives. I thought of Square Lamartine and of the fountain that was right in front of me, but already no longer so. What in Egypt had seemed a dream had come to life, only to slip back into my dreamworld.

Perhaps, I thought, in a few days it would help to look back on this very moment, when I was still enjoying myself in Paris and was still unaware of the sorrow that inevitably comes from looking back at this fountain. Perhaps, by rehearsing all this in advance, I might even, in some strange way, dull the pain. The fountain would stay, I would be gone. ("The days pass on, still I stay.") But at least I had anticipated it; at least I knew.

At the Gare de Lyon, my father boarded the train to say goodbye. He urged me not to be sad: there would be many more chances to visit. I looked out the window. I had no way of knowing that this was only the first time I would think I was seeing Paris for the last time.

For the next three years, following my Christmas, Easter, and summer vacations, I would find myself on the same exact platform on a Saturday evening, saying goodbye to Paris, worrying lest my father not get off the train in time, trying to convince myself this had indeed been our last visit, so as to ward off the hope and the disappointment when, later in Rome, I would catch myself longing to be in Paris, with nothing to turn to but my French books. In the days leading up to that parting moment at the Gare de Lyon, I would ask for very little of Paris—just a replay of my original heady two weeks. Like Stendhal, who would drop a little twig in a spring in

Salzburg and return months later to find it covered with speckling crystals, I too would return to Paris to find that the memory of my first visit had been thoroughly crystallized in Square Lamartine.

Not a day went by that I failed to log my impressions there, the better to remember them in Rome, knowing that, by cheating Paris of its magic, by numbing the pleasure of the moment with constant reminders of the unavoidable trip back, I was mitigating, if not averting, the shock of departure. It was my way of preempting tomorrow's worries by making tomorrow seem yesterday, of warding off adversity by warding off happiness as well. In the end, I learned not to enjoy going to Paris, or even to enjoy being there— because I enjoyed it too much.

What drove my brother insane were precisely these in-a-week-from-now-we'll-be-in-Rome-remembering-everything-we-said-and-did-in-Paris antics of mine. I was like a dying man taking detailed mental notes of sunlight, faces, foods, places, emotions, not only to remember them better when he reaches the hereafter, but to give himself the impression that he is still rooted in the present, still able to leave a patch, an afterimage, like one of those shadows imprinted on the bridges of Hiroshima. To this day my brother knows Paris better than I ever will, although I know one tiny corner better than most Parisians. The Paris I cultivated was a Paris one need not stay too long in. It was a Paris made to be yearned for and remembered, a Paris for the mind, a Paris which stood for the true life, the life done over, the better life, the one flooded in limelight, with tinsel, soundtrack, and costume. The life perhaps we don't think we deserve and aren't quite ready for and therefore never learn to want badly enough and put off grasping in the hope that, when we're not looking, when we've stopped hoping and thinking and dreaming, driven out of its hiding place, it might finally decide to tap us on the shoulder and beckon to us with a promise of bliss. We call it the romance of Paris.

My passage to France is no longer easy. I can *go* to France. But I can no longer *be* in France. To be in France is to think of all the times I came so close and failed, of near-misses and close calls. Emily Dickinson's "Except the heaven had come so near" rings in my ears each time I forget that perhaps I shouldn't try.

As soon as I arrive in Paris, I perform what I like to call my errands in time: I go back to all my private shrines and touch them as though to make sure they're still there, to placate them as one might a relative who is in a catatonic state but who you suspect is grateful you bothered to come at all. You touch, knowing there will be no response from them— or sensation on your part. As far as the city is concerned, you don't exist.

Once. revisiting Paris many years later, one evening, on the way to my Paris hotel, I heard a voice behind me and turned to see a girl no older than nineteen come out of the dark and ask the question I would have given anything to hear a woman say. I shrank back, as one does with a beggar who has come too close and to whom one hands a coin without touching hands. I had long ago learned to prefer the imagined encounter, or the memory of the imagined encounter, to the thing itself.

Now, whenever I say goodbye to Paris, I do so without making trouble. At the airport I do not think this is the last time I'll ever return. I am, I tell myself, happy to be going home. I open a book, talk to my fellow passengers, watch the news. I never, ever look back. Am I aware that the loves we decline to look back upon are those we are not certain we have overcome? In that sense, Lot was far guiltier than his wife: fleeing Sodom and Gomorrah, she simply turned her head; he made it a point not to.

A few years ago I called a close friend in France to let her know that my wife and I would be coming to Paris that Christmas.

After she picked up the receiver, I asked her how Paris was. Her answer did not come as a surprise: "Gray. Paris is always gray these days. It never changes." That of course is exactly how I remember Paris. "And how is New York?" she asked. She missed New York. "Sunny," I said, "as on any winter day." She missed winter in New York, said she missed coming out of the subway at West Fourth. Balducci's, Bleecker Street, and finally Horatio Street, where, years ago, she'd looked out of her windows facing West Street and liked to imagine . . . well, Paris. We laughed. And suddenly, as I was listening to her, I caught myself missing Horatio Street as well, as if it, too, had been taken from me, though it was a subway ride away.

I was, not where she was, but where she wanted to be, though where I thought I wanted to be was precisely where she was—and perhaps that's also what I wanted: to be where she was, longing for Horatio Street so that I could suddenly turn around and tell myself: But I am near Horatio Street, I like being in New York. I distance myself from things by alleging they're unreachable, only so as to allow them to think I've given up on them and that they should let their guard down, and then, when they least expect it, I pounce . . .

In my usual manner I said I did not like traveling, I never found Paris relaxing, I would much rather stay in New York and imagine having wonderful dinners in Paris. "Yes, of course," she agreed, already annoyed. "Since you're going to Paris, you don't want to go to Paris. But if you were staying in New York, you'd want to be in Paris. But since you're not staying, but going, just do me a favor." Exasperation bristled in her voice. "When you're in Paris, think of yourself in New York longing for Paris, and everything will be fine."

And that is precisely what I did. My wife and I walked around, went to the stores, visited this or that place. But the one thing I wanted to do—namely, return to the Paris of my adolescence—I kept delaying, because I could not rest until I had done it but did not want to do it too soon. I knew that once I had revisited my sites, Paris would hold no further interest for me.

My wife was far from unfamiliar with this Paris of mine. I had brought her there ten years earlier on our honeymoon, and again three years later with our then-ten-month-old son. I had wanted to show her the house where my great-aunt lived, and the walks we sometimes took together, and the fountain where I would go with empty bottles to watch the girls.

I still remember how, on the first day of our honeymoon in Paris, walking along the grand avenues of the 16th arrondissement, staring at the lit-up buildings with their promise of intimate gatherings, I had begun to tell my wife about my first sojourn in Paris and of my thwarted love for the city to which I would return so often during my years in Rome, each time summoning up the memory of my prior visit or anticipating my next, leaving almost no room for the visit itself. We walked to the place de Barcelone, stood and faced Pont de Grenelle, not far from Pont Mirabeau, and I pointed out the small-scale Statue of Liberty that is a reverse imitation of the one in New York, thinking to myself how things get boxed into each other and how cities and bridges and parks, like far-flung cousins, become mirror images of their replicas.

When we reached La Muette, one of my favorite spots, I told my wife about the royal falcon house after which the neighborhood is named—from the verb *muer*, to molt—and of how, centuries ago, this was where the king's birds were brought each year to shed their feathers. As we walked, I began to wonder what the opposite of molting was and why, unlike the body, which sheds everything, the soul cannot let go of anything but compiles and accumulates, growing annual rings around the things it wants and dreams of and remembers. I already knew that in years to come I would turn back to this very evening at La Muette and remember how I had come there with my wife on our honeymoon and how, with her, I had remembered the young man who had walked these same sidewalks trying to find a Paris he did not know he had invented.

And now, here we are on the same spot, no longer newlyweds, thinking to ourselves how much and how very little things have changed since our last visit. We are having a late lunch, in the exact same café on the Place du Trocadéro where we lunched a decade ago, and without thinking we have ended up ordering the same meal. I suspect my wife knows where we are headed, though I have not told her yet, as I haven't told her that we are to visit not just the old building where my great-aunt lived but the tiny park as well.

The sky as always is a silver gray, and the city is in full ferment as we leave the café down the unavoidable route toward the old apartment. I recognize the silence that descends over that wonderful corner of the 16th arrondissement late on a weekday afternoon as children come home from school, bookbags and all, accompanied by a cluster of babysitters who trail behind as their charges scamper quietly ahead. And there—I do it each time—I look up to the fifth floor, where my great-aunt and my grandmother used to live. I can still remember the last time I visited this building with my wife.

Of course, as my wife and I both know, I have already recorded that selfsame visit in a memoir. What makes the present situation all the more uncanny is that earlier today, wandering into one of my favorite foreign-language bookshops on the rue de Rivoli, I had asked for the book—with studied nonchalance, as authors do. I wanted to find out whether they had the British paperback edition, which I had never seen. The salesclerk, who had no idea who I was, turned out to be familiar with the title but reported she could not locate the book on the shelves. I was browsing in another section entirely when suddenly she came rushing up. "Monsieur, I've found it!" Damn! Now I had to purchase my own book, or give away the fact that I had been "testing" the store.

So here I am, two hours later, walking with my own book in my hand in front of a building described in that very same book, feeling like Don Quixote in the second part of his novel, or like Saint-Simon holding in his hand the vile character portrait he had penned of the person on whom he was now lavishing compliment after compliment. I feel nothing. My wife, who in my book asks, "Didn't you ever want to go upstairs to visit?" does not speak her lines, and I cannot remember mine and clearly do not want to be caught looking them up now. So we leave the scene quite unsatisfied, knowing we will probably never do this again.

I ask my wife if she minds taking a walk around the vest-pocket park stuck in between the grand turn-of-the-century buildings. I feel like a child asking his harried parents to stop at the window of yet another toy store. But I am taking too long, I do not know what I am looking for, we are both jet-lagged and tired, and any moment now it may start raining. And still no epiphany, nothing, just this rushed, desultory prowling around what seems to be a little fountain in a *petit square* that long ago was named Place Victor-Hugo and then became Square Lamartine. What was I looking for, anyway? Crestfallen, I accompany my wife to the nearest metro station. I had thought the park would remind me of a similar one in New York.

Four days after our perfunctory visit, on the eve of our departure, I decide to come back alone. I make my rounds again, scouring the scene, trying to squeeze out a droplet of sensation. Nothing. All I remember is coming here four days earlier. It is five o'clock. I could—and the thought races through my mind before I can check it in time—call ahead and then go upstairs for tea.

A summer later I returned to Square Lamartine, this time with my seven-year-old son. I showed him where I had lived when I was seven years older than he, trying to explain to myself that, though he was far closer to how old I was then, I had, contrary to all appearances, scarcely turned a new leaf since. I took pictures of him in front of my great-aunt's building, just as I had done with my wife on our honeymoon, then walked around a bit, snapping the park, the adjoining buildings, him playing in the tiny enclosure by the sandbox, knowing that one day, his passage here, like my wife's, my brother's, my father's, my great-aunt's, and mine would find a place in this concentric planisphere named Square Lamartine.

My son is playing in the park. There is, of course, no way for him to know what I am thinking. But I am standing there the way my father did when he would take me as a child to his father's grave in Alexandria because there was no one he would rather be with at that moment. Except that, in my case, I have accompanied my son not so much to a gravesite as to the resting place of a part of my life that was never even lived, a chapter written in invisible ink. In Lamartine's garden I am still combing the scene, looking for ancient relics and clues, not just memories but generations of memories, deep, artesian memories, the way police inspectors in the movies pick up hair, nails, and lint and drop them with tweezers into a plastic bag, the way people scour the beaches on summer evenings looking for jewelry that was lost not just that day but many summers before.

As I stare at this tiny park, I think to myself of all I have logged away and why I always feel as though nothing, even when written, remains fixed for too long before it starts to rise from the page, as if it had been but figuratively buried in paper and now aches for life again.

And while thinking of all this, I suddenly remember a literary character I have not brought to mind since leaving Italy three decades ago. It is a character named Astolph from *Orlando Furioso*, the sixteenth-century epic poem by Ariosto. This Astolph lands on the moon—in the poem, a giant lost-and-found, bric-a-brac landscape containing everything that was ever lost or ever wished for but never granted. Mankind's unrealized artifacts litter the lunar surface, and you must thread your way cautiously through the rubble, for vials containing stolen goods and unhatched schemes crackle underfoot, and wasted years and abandoned hopes are strewn about everywhere.

Like Astolph wandering in search of the flask that contains the sanity misplaced by Ariosto's hero Orlando, what I knew I would find here in this quiet landscape was my whole Paris: the crowded Citroën with my cousins—it was there—the hunt for Bach's double concerto—it, too, was there—my love for the metro, Apollinaire's poem, the Bogart revival, the smell of cigarettes and damp wool coats, the girls whose gaze was unlike any I had met before, the woman who finally came out of the dark only to be shooed away, the plays, the brasseries, the books, down to the late-afternoon tea I had conjured the day I came without my wife and thought I was a phone call away from people who had died so long ago, the light drizzle on silver-gray days when Paris is awash in traffic lights, my first walk down by the royal falcon house, the day it finally dawned on me that my life had not even started, or that life, like Paris, was little else than a collection of close calls and near-misses, and that the objects I loved and would never outgrow and wished to take with me would always litter this landscape, because they were lost or had never existed, because even the life I had yearned to live when looking out the window with my great-aunt in Alexandria and dreaming of a Seine scarcely seven minutes away was also cast upon this landscape, a past life, a pluperfect life, a conditional life, a life made, like Paris, for the mind. Or for paper.

Letter from Illiers-Combray:

In Search of Proust

→‖←

It was by train that I had always imagined arriving in Illiers-Combray—not just any train, but one of those drafty, pre–World War I, rattling wagons which I like to think still leave Paris early every morning and, after hours of swaying through the countryside, squeak their way into a station that is as old and weather-beaten as all of yesteryear's provincial stops in France. The picture in my mind was always the same: the train would come to a wheezing halt and release a sudden loud chuff of steam; a door would slam open; someone would call out Illiers-Combray; and, finally, like the young Marcel Proust arriving for his Easter vacation just over a century ago, I would step down nervously into the small, turn-of-the-century town in Eure-et-Loir which he described so lovingly in *A la recherche du temps perdu*.

Instead, when I finally made my way to Illiers-Combray, I arrived by car with Anne Borrel, the curator of the Proust Museum there, who had offered to pick me up at my Paris hotel that morning. In my pocket was a cheap and tattered Livre de Poche edition of *Du côté de chez Swann* which I had brought in the hope that I'd find a moment to read some of my favorite passages on holy ground. That was to be my way of closing the loop, of coming home to a book I had first opened more than thirty years earlier.

I had bought it with my father, when I was fifteen, one summer evening in Paris. We were taking a long walk, and as we passed a small restaurant I told him that the overpowering smell of refried food reminded me of the tanneries along the coast road outside Alexandria, in Egypt. He said he hadn't thought of it that way, but, yes, I was right, the restaurant did smell like a tannery. And as we began working our way back through strands of shared memories—the tanneries, the beaches, the ruined Roman temple west of Alexandria, our summer beach house—all this suddenly made him think of Proust. Had I read Proust? he asked. No, I hadn't. Well, perhaps I should. My father said this with a sense of urgency, so unlike him that he immediately tempered it, for fear I'd resist the suggestion simply because it was a parent's.

The next day, sitting in the sun on a metal chair in Square Lamartine, I opened Proust for the first time. That evening, when my father asked how I had liked what I'd read, I feigned indifference, not really knowing whether I intended to spite a father who wanted me to love the author he loved most or to spite an author who had come uncomfortably close. For in the eighty-odd pages I had read that day I had rediscovered my entire childhood in Alexandria: the impassive cook, my bad-tempered aunts and skittish friends, the buzz of flies on sunny afternoons spent reading indoors when it was too hot outside, dinners in the garden with scant lights to keep mosquitoes away, the "ferruginous, interminable" peal of the garden bell announcing the occasional night guest who, like Charles Swann, came uninvited but whom everyone had nevertheless been expecting. Every year, thousands of Prousto-tourists come to the former Illiers, which extended its name in honor of Proust's fictional town Combray, in 1971, on the centennial of his birth. The town knows it, proclaims it, milks it.

Today, Illiers-Combray sells around two thousand madeleine pastries a month. The shell-shaped cakes are displayed in the windows of pastry shops like propitiatory offerings to an unseen god and are sold by the dozen—in case one wants to take some home to friends or relatives, the way pilgrims take back holy water from the Jordan or an olive twig from Gethsemane.

For the reader on a Proustian pilgrimage, tasting a madeleine is the supreme tribute to Proust. (As no *pâtisserie* fails to remind the tourists, it was on tasting a madeleine, now the most famous sponge cake in the history of world literature, that the adult narrator of Proust's novel was transported to his boyhood days in Combray.) It is also a gesture of communion through which readers hope, like Proust, to come home to something bigger, more solid, and ultimately, perhaps, truer than fiction itself. Anne Borrel often tells these Proust groupies that the cult of the madeleine is blasphemous, as are the claims made by one of the *pâtissiers* that members of the *famille* Proust used to purchase their madeleines on his premises. (In earlier drafts of the novel, Proust's madeleines may have been slices of melba toast, which evolved into toasted bread, only later to metamorphose into the sponge cakes.) But no one listens. Besides, going to Illiers-Combray and not tasting a madeleine would be like going to Jerusalem and not seeing the Western Wall, or to Greenwich and not checking your watch. Luckily, I was able to resist temptation: during my visit, on a Sunday just a few days before Christmas, all the pastry shops were closed. Before going to the Proust Museum, Anne Borrel and I had lunch at a tiny restaurant called Le Samovar. Plump and middle-aged, Borrel is the author of a cookbook and culinary history titled *Dining with Proust*. She told me that some of the tourists come from so far away and have waited so long to make the trip that as soon as they step into Proust's house they burst into tears. I pictured refugees getting off a ship and kneeling to kiss the beachhead. I asked about Proust's suddenly increasing popularity. "Proust," Borrel replied, "is a must." (She repeated these four words, like a verdict, several times during the day.) She reminded me that there were currently six French editions of *A la recherche du temps perdu* in print. I told her that a fourth English-language edition was due to appear in 2001. And that wasn't all: trade books on Proust and coffee-table iconographies were everywhere; in Paris, I had seen at least half a dozen new books that bore Proust's name or drew on Proustian characters occupying precious space on the display tables of bookstores and department stores. Even Proust's notes, manuscripts, and publishing history had been deemed complicated enough to warrant a book of their own, called *Remembrance of Publishers Past*. Add to that T-shirts, watches, CDs, concerts, videos, scarves, posters, books on tape, newsletters, and a comic-strip version entitled *Combray*, whose first printing, of twelve thousand copies, sold out in three weeks. Not to mention the 1997–98 convention in Liège celebrating the seventy-fifth anniversary of Proust's death, with sessions on music and Proust, eating and Proust, a writing competition (on the subject of "Time Lost and Time Regained"), and a colloquium on asthma and allergies.

This kaleidoscope of Proustophernalia is matched by as many testimonials and tributes to Proust, in which he takes many forms. There is Proust the élitist and high-society snob; Proust the son of a Jewish mother; Proust the loner; Proust the dandy; Proust the analytical aesthete; Proust the soulful, lovelorn boy; Proust the tart, the dissembling coquette; the Belle Epoque Proust; the professional whiner; the prankster; the subversive classicist; the eternal procrastinator; and the asthmatic, hypochondriacal Proust. But the figure who lies at the heart of today's Proust revival is the intimate Proust, the Proust who perfected the studied unveiling of spontaneous feelings. Proust invented a language, a style, a rhythm, and a vision that gave memory and introspection an aesthetic scope and magnitude no author had conferred on either before. He allowed intimacy itself to become an art form. This is not to say that the vertiginous spate of memoirs that have appeared recently, with their de rigueur regimens of child, spouse, and substance abuse, owe their existence, their voice, or their sensibility to Proust— clearly, they owe far more to Freud. But it does help to explain why Proust is more popular today, in the age of the memoir, than he has been at any other time in the century.

Like every great memoirist who has had a dizzying social life and a profoundly lonely one, Proust wrote because writing was his way of both reaching for an ever-elusive world and securing his distance from it. He was among the first writers in this century to disapprove of the critics' tendency to seek correspondences between an artist's work and his private life. The slow, solitary metamorphosis of what truly happened into what, after many years, finally emerges in prose is the hallmark of Proust's labor of love. Proust is at once the most canonical and the most uncanonical author, the most solemnly classical and the most subversive, the author in whom farce and lyricism, arrogance and humility, beauty and revulsion are indissolubly fused, and whose ultimate contradiction reflects an irreducible fact about all of us: we are driven by something as simple and as obvious as the desire to be happy, and, if that fails, by the belief that we once have been.

My conversation with Anne Borrel was interrupted by the arrival of customers outside Le Samovar. "Take a look at those four," Borrel said, pointing to two couples dawdling at the entrance. "I'll bet you anything they're *proustiens.*" She referred to all tourists as *proustiens*—meaning not Proust scholars but individuals whom the French like to call *les amis de Proust*, Proustologues, Proustolaters, Proustocentrics, Proustomaniacs, Proustophiles, Proustophiliacs, Proustoholics . . . or fiddles (to use a term dear to Proust's malevolent archsnob, Mme Verdurin). One of the four opened the door of the restaurant and asked in a thick Spanish accent whether lunch was still being served. "*Pintades*"—guinea hens—"are all that's left," snapped the owner of Le Samovar. Borrel and I exchanged a complicitous glance, because talk of fowl immediately brought to mind a discussion we'd had in the car about Proust's servant Françoise, who in *Swann's Way* butchers a chicken and then curses it for not dying fast enough.

The four tourists were shown to a table. One asked the proprietor what time the Proust Museum would open that afternoon, and he regretfully informed them that the museum was closed for the holidays. They were crestfallen. "What a pity! And we've come all the way from Argentina."

Anne Borrel had heard every word of the exchange. She reminded me of a teacher who with her back turned to the class while she's writing on the blackboard knows exactly who's whispering what to whom. She leaned over and told one of the Argentines, "You may have come to the right place." Overjoyed, the Argentine blurted out, "You mean Marcel Proust used to eat here, in this restaurant?" "No," Borrel answered, smiling indulgently. She told them that an improvised tour of the house could be arranged after coffee, and the Argentines went back to talking softly about Proust, staring every once in a while at our table with the thrilled and wary gaze of people who have been promised a miracle.

By the time our coffee was served, we had also acquired two English and three French *proustiens*, and a warm, festive mood permeated Le Samovar. It was like the gathering of pilgrims in Chaucer's Tabard Inn. Introductions were unnecessary. We knew why we were there, and we all had a tale to tell.

By then, some of us would have liked nothing more than a fireplace, a large cognac, and a little prodding to induce us to recount how we had first come to read Proust, to love Proust, how Proust had changed our lives. I was, it dawned on me, among my own. After dessert, Borrel put on her coat. *"On y va?"* she asked, rattling a giant key chain that bore a bunch of old keys with long shafts and large, hollowed oval heads. She led us down the rue du Docteur Proust, named after Proust's father, who by the turn of the century had helped to halt the spread of cholera in Europe. The sidewalks and streets were empty. Everyone seemed to be away for the holidays. Franco-jazz Muzak emanated from loudspeakers, mounted on various lampposts, that were apparently intended to convey a festive Yule spirit, but otherwise Illiers-Combray was deserted and gray—a dull, cloying, humdrum, wintry, ashen town, where the soul could easily choke. Small wonder that Marcel developed asthma, or that he had the heebie-jeebies on returning home after long evening walks with his parents, knowing that by the time dinner was served life would hold no surprises—only the inevitable walk up the creepy staircase and that frightful drama called bed-time. Borrel stopped at one of many nondescript doors along the empty street. She stared at it for a moment, almost as though she were trying to remember whether this was indeed the right address, then took out her keys, inserted one into the lock, and suddenly gave it a vigorous turn, yanking the door open.

"C'est ici que tout commence," she said. One by one, we filed into Proust's garden. Fortunately, no one cried.

Borrel pointed to a little bell at the top of the gate. I couldn't contain myself. "Could this be the ferruginous bell?" I asked. It was a question she'd heard before. She took a breath. "You mean not the large and noisy rattle which deafened with its ferruginous, interminable, frozen sound any member of the household who set it off by coming in 'without ringing,' but the double peal, 'timid, oval, gilded,' of the visitor's bell, whereupon everyone would exclaim, 'A visitor! Who on earth could it be?' " (She was quoting from memory, and every time one of us asked a question after that she would recite the answer.) Next she led us into the restored, relatively humble middle-class house—by no means the large villa I'd always imagined. The kitchen, where I'd envisaged Françoise cooking the chicken she had viciously butchered, was a sunless alcove. The dining room, with a small round table and dark wood paneling, was a depressing melee of browns. Then we came to Marcel's bedroom, with its tiny Empire-style bed, the magic lantern that kept him company at night when he dreaded sleep, and nearby the George Sand novel bound in red. In another room was the sofa that Proust had given to his maid Céleste Albaret, which her daughter had donated to the museum—and was perhaps the inspiration for the fictional sofa that Marcel inherited from his Tante Léonie, made love on, and eventually passed along to the owner of a brothel.

When Borrel indicated another room, on the second floor, I interrupted her to suggest that it must surely be the room where, under lock and key, Marcel discovered the secret pleasures of onanism. Borrel neither confirmed nor denied my allegation. She said only, " 'The little room that smelt of orrisroot . . . [where] I explored, across the bounds of my own experience, an untrodden path which I thought was deadly.' " In this way, I was summarily put in my place—for presuming to show off and for implying that I could make obvious what Proust's oblique words had made explicit enough.

Back in the garden, I told her that the way she had opened the main door had reminded me of the moment in the novel when, after a long, moonlit family walk, Marcel's father pretends to be lost. Everyone in our group suddenly remembered the episode, and, excited, one of the Englishmen described it to his friend, explaining that it was only after making everyone else panic in the dark that Marcel's father had finally taken a key out of his pocket and quietly inserted it in what the others until then had failed to see was the back gate to their very own house. According to the Englishman, Marcel's admiring mother, stunned by her husband's ability to save the day, had exclaimed, "*Tu es fantastique!*"

"*Tu es extraordinaire!*" Borrel corrected him.

I had always liked that scene: the family wandering in the moonlight, the boy and his mother convinced that they're lost, the father teasing them. It reminded me of the way Proust's sentences roam and stray through a labyrinth of words and clauses, only to turn around—just when you are about to give up—and show you something you had always suspected but had never put into words. The sentences tell you that you haven't really drifted far at all, and that real answers may not always be obvious but aren't really hidden, either. Things, he reminds us, are never as scary as we thought they were, nor are we ever as stranded or as helpless as we feared.

Borrel left us for a moment to check on something inside the museum, and we spent some time discussing our favorite Proust passages. We all wondered which gate Swann's prototype would come through in the evenings, and where the aunts had been sitting when they refused to thank him for his gift but finally consented to say something so indirect that Swann failed to realize that they actually were thanking him.

"It all seems so small," said the Englishman, who was visibly disappointed by the house. My thoughts drifted to a corner of the garden. The weather was growing colder, and yet I was thinking of Marcel's summer days, and of my own summer days as well, and of the garden where, deaf to the world, I had found myself doing what Proust described in his essay "On Reading":

> giving more attention and tenderness to characters in books than to people in real life, not always daring to admit how much I loved them . . . those people, for whom I had panted and sobbed, and whom, at the close of the book, I would never see again, and no longer know anything about . . . I would have wanted so much for these books to continue, and if that were impossible, to have other information on all those characters, to learn now something about their lives, to devote mine to things that might not be entirely foreign to the love they had inspired in me and whose object I was suddenly missing . . . beings who tomorrow would be but names on a forgotten page, in a book having no connection with life.

The guided tour took more than two hours. It ended, as all guided tours do, in the gift shop. The guests were kindly reminded that, despite the impromptu nature of today's visit, they shouldn't forget to pay for their tickets. Everyone dutifully scrambled to buy Proust memorabilia. I toyed with the idea of a Proust watch on whose dial were inscribed the opening words of *A la recherche du temps perdu:* "*Longtemps, je me suis couché de bonne heure.*" But I knew I'd never wear it. The visitors began talking of heading back to Paris. I was almost tempted to hitch a ride with one of them, but Borrel had promised to take me for a night walk through the streets of Illiers-Combray and then accompany me to the train station. The others stood idly about in the evening air, obviously reluctant to put Illiers-Combray behind them. They exchanged addresses and telephone numbers. "Proust is a must," I heard the Argentine say, an infatuated giggle in his voice. When Borrel left the shop to lock the back door, I was suddenly alone.

As I looked out the window at the garden where the Proust family had dined on warm summer evenings, I was seized with a strange premonition of asthma. How could Marcel have ever loved such a place? Or had he never loved it? Had he loved only the act of returning to it on paper, because that was how he lived his life— first by wanting to live it, and later by remembering having wanted to, and ultimately by writing about the two? The part in between— the actual living—was what had been lost. Proust's garden was little more than a place where he had once yearned to be elsewhere— never the primal scene or the ground zero. Illiers itself was simply a place where the young Proust dreamed of a better life to come. But, because the dream never came true, he had learned to love instead the place where the dream was born. That life did happen, and happened so intensely, to someone who seemed so reluctant to live it is part of the Proustian miracle.

This is the irony that greets all Proust pilgrims: they go in search of things that Proust remembered far better than he had ever really known them, and which he yearned to recover more than he had ever loved them. In the end, like the boy mentioned by Freud who liked to lose things because he enjoyed finding them, Proust realized that he couldn't write about anything unless he thought he had lost it first. Perhaps I, too, had come here in order to lose Combray, if only to rediscover it in the pages I knew I would read on the way home.

My train wasn't due for an hour and a half, and Anne Borrel invited me to have a cup of tea at her house before our walk. We closed the door to the museum and set off down dark and deserted alleys.

"Illiers gets so empty," she said, sighing.

"It must be lonely," I said.

"It has its pluses."

Her house was bigger than Proust's and had a far larger garden and orchard. This seemed odd to me—like finding that the gate-keeper owns a faster car and has better central heating than the owner of the palace.

As we headed back to the train station after our tea, I walked quickly. Borrel tried to stop long enough to show me the spot where the Prousts had returned from their Sunday promenades, but I didn't want to miss my connection to Paris. It seemed a shame that, after so many years, this longed-for moonlit walk, so near at hand, should be the very thing I'd forfeit. But the last thing I needed was to be sentenced to a sleepless night in Proust's boy-hood town. I alluded to a possible next time. Borrel mentioned spring, when Proust's favorite flower, the hawthorn, would be in bloom. But I knew, and perhaps she knew, too, that I had no plan to return.

On my way to Paris, I skimmed through the pages of "Com-bray," the first chapter of *In Search of Lost Time.* As I read about the steeples of Martinville or Tante Léonie, eternally perched in her bedroom, on the first floor, overlooking rue Saint-Jacques, it occurred to me that I had rushed back to the book not to verify the existence of what I had just seen but to make certain that those places I remembered and loved as though my own childhood had been spent among them had not been altered by the reality of the dull, tile-roofed town shown to me by Anne Borrel. I wanted to return to my first reading of Proust—the way, after seeing a film based on a novel, we struggle to resurrect our private portrait of its characters and their world, only to find that the images we've treasured for so long have vanished, like ancient frescoes exposed to daylight by a thoughtless archaeologist. Would my original image of a stone villa with a spacious dining room and a wide staircase leading to the child's solitary bedroom be able to withstand the newly discovered little house with its squeaky wooden stairwell and drab, sunless rooms? And could this tawdry garden really be the glorious place where Marcel read away entire afternoons on a wicker chair under a chestnut tree, lost to the voices of those calling him inside and to the hourly chime of the church of Saint-Hilaire—whose real name, as I had found out that day, was not Saint-Hilaire but Saint-Jacques, which, moreover, was not really the name of the street watched over by Tante Léonie, who, it turned out, was herself more likely to have been an uncle.

Inside the sepia cover of *Swann's Way* I searched also for the sense of wonder I had brought to it that summer evening more than thirty years before, when I'd had the good fortune to be with a man who was the first person to mention Proust to me and who, because he was unable to give me so many things then, had only this to give me, and gave it tentatively, self-consciously, as though he were giving part of himself, as he told me about Proust—how Proust remembered things that everyone else seemed to forget, how he saw through people, though they still managed to fool him, and how he did all those things in sentences that were ever so long—and steered me, as we rushed to buy the first volume before the stores closed, to a writer I have since loved above all others, not just because of who he was and what he wrote, or because of who I became the more I read him, but because on that late-summer evening I already knew I had just received, perhaps without my father's knowing it, his dearest, most enduring gift of love.

In the Muslim City

of Bethlehem

❖

The rain falls on Bethlehem under a light-gray morning sky as fleets of tourist buses creep up the dusty slope leading to Manger Square. The area is crowded with people, pushcarts, and parked vehicles, and the buses must thread their way between rows of taxis before finding a place to unload passengers. The last bus, far older than the rest, looks as if only a miracle could have got its weather-beaten carcass up the hill to Bethlehem. Its pilgrims look weather-beaten, too, and as they mass on the street waiting for their guide, who is arguing with a guide from another tourist company, to usher them to the holy sites, they look uneasily across Manger Square. All of them are wearing the glazed, startled look of people who are at once awed, tired, and disappointed. The Bethlehem they have found looks nothing like the town God's son might want to be born in. But that's the whole point. Everything here is meant to test one's faith.

The pilgrims, mostly women, will soon recover from the shock, but as they take in the unfamiliar place, with its light rain and glistening pavement teeming with boys who scurry about Manger Square brandishing open and mostly broken umbrellas for the tourists, they cannot believe that this may be the holiest moment in their lives. This, the most un-Christmaslike spot in Christendom, is what they will take with them and remember. Many will come to celebrate Christmas this year, as so many pilgrims do, but the festivities will have a different tenor: barring some last-minute hitch, this is the first time in twenty-eight years that Bethlehem will celebrate Christmas without an Israeli presence.

A traditional Midnight Mass is celebrated in the Church of St. Catherine every Christmas Eve and broadcast worldwide. But now that the Israelis have decided to hand over the city to Palestinian authorities a week before Christmas, "maybe they'll have big celebrations," says Itzhak, a Jerusalem cabby whom I summon by cellular phone.

I ask whether he really believes this. Itzhak snickers. "The Christians are leaving," he says. The implication is clear: they're afraid of the Muslims. Everyone knows, but no one says it: the Christians are the Jews of Bethlehem.

Itzhak is not only a driver but an amateur historian who doubles as a tour guide, which he does by holding on to the steering wheel with one hand and pointing freely with the other, constantly turning around to look you in the face as he expounds on the more subtle aspects of Jewish history. In the end, it seemed safer to sit next to him. He is a burly sort with a thick mustache, deep voice, and muscular body. He speaks good English, has an instinct for wit and paradox, and knows a proverb for every occasion. When he tried to temper my fears of going to Bethlehem by uttering a proverb, I almost said, "Enough with proverbs." Then I remembered that Sancho Panza had a proverb against proverbs, too.

Like the pilgrim women from the small bus, I, too, am thinking of another Bethlehem, of the one I learned about from Christmas carols. Of distant, imagined evenings draped in snow that is always deep and crisp and even, and of that medieval village that rises in our fantasy each year for at least twelve days, the way a tree inevitably rises in every living room, even in my own, though I am Jewish. It is not so much Christmas I celebrate as that aura of peace, which lasts no longer than my tree, but a peace that I anticipate for months and sometimes lose before even finding it.

I think of the carols I learned long ago in Egypt, carols I still love but that seem so out of place here, even in these incense-ridden churches, which are bleak, tense, medieval, and cruel. And I think, too, of the word "Bethlehem" and of the strange place it acquired in the bowdlerized lyrics we used in school in Egypt, where "Bethlehem" replaced another three-syllable word that had suddenly disappeared from our Christmas carols. We sang "Born is the king of Bethlehem," not "of Israel."

Bethlehem is poor, dirty, shabby. It is the smells I recognize. A small café on Manger Square, located under a large pine, is called the Christmas Tree, It gives off a smell of skewered-meat sandwiches, of falafel and coffee. It is well situated and the owner, a Christian, has obviously done well. But he paid a price for refusing to close his business during a general strike. Islamic fundamentalists burned his car and bombed his home. I am tempted to order a sandwich, but think twice about doing so.

Not five steps away from the Christmas Tree is the town's largest mosque. Behind it is Friday's open-air market, crammed with a slovenly array of fruits and vegetables hanging from shops, pushcarts, and portable stalls. Vendors scream out their produce, and women lug heavy loads home, howling at children who have strayed too far, while clusters of men sit around, some doing nothing, others arguing, everyone smoking. A vendor wearing the traditional kaffiyeh is talking on a cellular phone. A small boy has just delivered coffee to three old men and is respectfully kissing the hand of the eldest. A shopkeeper is trying to tape two Santas to his store window. Inside another shop a young man sits cross-legged, wearing only one sneaker; the other shoe is in the hands of an old cobbler trying to sew a torn seam. The tiny barbershop is empty—except for the barber, who reads on his barber seat. Outside the shop, seven youths stand against a wall, idling New York–style.

"This is Bethlehem?" I blurt out to my driver.

"This is Bethlehem," he replies spiritedly, as though to ask, What did you expect—Jerusalem? Indeed, Bethlehem is not more than twenty minutes from Jerusalem, whose outline we can still see; yet it seems worlds away.

On another day I am driven to Bethlehem by a cabby named Moishe. We had agreed that he would drop me off at Manger Square and go back to the outskirts of the city to wait for my telephone call when I was finished meeting with Elias Freij, the mayor of Bethlehem. This was my idea, not Moishe's. He would have waited at Manger Square the whole time, probably near the Israeli police station, which is surrounded by a high barbed-wire fence.

No sooner has he left with his car than a man in his mid-sixties approaches me. "And this is the basilica of the Nativity," he breaks in, as if we had already been speaking for hours. "And my name is George. And I am Christian. And please, this way," he adds, warning me not to trip as we enter the church through the Door of Humility. The entrance, he explains, was purposely narrowed to prevent people from riding horses into the church, as well as to force them to bow as they enter. When we are inside, he asks where

I come from. I know what he is really asking, and I don't want to tell him. I say I am from America, but I don't mention New York. Nor do I tell him I was born in Egypt. He would deduce that I am Jewish, and I don't want anyone to know—not when I feel I am probably the only Jew in a place where all the other Jews are safely ensconced behind a barbed-wire fence that stretches around the police compound.

George hands me a taper. When I search my pocket, he motions me not to. I ignite the taper with a lighted candle and wedge it in place among others on a tiny crammed candle stand, thinking of a custom a Greek Orthodox nanny had taught me in Alexandria when you want to make a wish or mourn the dead.

Meanwhile, a contingent of women from South America has arrived. The women lie down next to the fourteen-pronged silver star of Bethlehem embedded in the stone floor, marking the spot where Jesus was said to be born. They will be shown the altar of the manger, then the place where the Magi laid their presents down, light a few tapers, and, holding hands, band together around the altar of Christ's birth and sing lullabies to the child Jesus.

As the group prepares to step into the adjoining cloister of the Church of St. Catherine, it is clearly time for me to get rid of George. Impossible. And would I really leave Bethlehem without seeing the church bell? he asks. The bell, as it turns out, is best seen from an alley where, as if by chance, I am led to a small souvenir shop. This was bound to happen. I am now sure that George is in cahoots with its owner. I am wrong. George is the owner. And I am not to feel I must buy something, he says. I scan the shop, feeling totally dispirited, still trying to make the best of things. After all, the business generated by tourism is what keeps Bethlehem alive. There are plenty of shops and factories devoted exclusively to the manufacture of Christian art and trinkets. But I cannot find a thing to buy here. I have rarely seen such ugly merchandise: inlaid mother-of-pearl boxes, sculptured candles that look like bloated human organs, and those carved, unpolished olive-wood statues of the manger, the Magi, and the Crucifixion.

Itzhak, my other cabby, has a theory about olive trees. Twisted, short, yet beautiful, they tie you to the land, he says, because they grow well in this dry, rocky landscape and can be transplanted easily. With olive trees, you could stake out land and make it your own, the way squatters are tied to their land, or the way parents are tied to their children or to each other through their children. During the Intifada, I remember watching on television a group of Arab villagers transplanting very young saplings. No sooner were their roots buried in the soil than an Israeli patrol car swooped into position and a foreman type got out, lumbered up to the two shoots, and yanked them out of the ground. The ban on growing things— or on begetting children—has an ancient history here, not irrelevant to Christmas.

The mayor of Bethlehem agrees with Itzhak's view of olive trees. The mayor should know. His family, I am told, owns olive groves and has done very well. But, the mayor adds when we're talking in his office, the trees shouldn't just tie you to the land. They should bind people together as well. Olives, I am reminded, are a symbol of peace. Mayor Freij dreams of a loose federation of Benelux-type states that will include Jordan, Palestine, and Israel. "Everyone must learn to live together since everyone is destined to live together," he says.

This implies that everyone should sit together at the same table and enjoy the meal. I wonder why no one has thought of it sooner—until I realize that, in this part of the world, the question is not how to sit three adversaries at the same table but how to sit them on the same chair. These are not just three nations or three religions; each has its subsidiary warring sects and, within each of these, ageless rivalries, fiercely and relentlessly petty, as everything is when God, pride, and land are at stake. Roman Catholics, Armenians, and the Greek Orthodox seldom agree about anything. Among ancient Jews, the same tussling consumed the Essenes, Pharisees, and Sadducees; it continues today among Jews who cannot even agree on what constitutes a Jew. Among Arabs, the bloody claims of the Shiites and Sunnis have wiped entire areas from the face of an earth that has no more cheeks to turn. As for the Christians of Bethlehem, they were so contentious among themselves that European nations were forced to intervene and take sides—a situation that fueled the outbreak of the Crimean War.

You have only to visit the Old City of Jerusalem to sense that even dust from one quarter hates dust from another. In the Church of the Holy Sepulchre, each corner is zealously guarded by a different sect, and the spite among them is legendary. Tourists would give anything to witness their brawls. In Bethlehem, the Church of the Nativity literally feeds into the Church of St. Catherine through a network of caves, but these churches are of different denominations; the first is Greek Orthodox, the other is Roman Catholic.

Everyone lives on top of one another, for the land belongs to no one, but there is no one to whom this land does not belong. In the language of the New Testament, the first ones here were the last to return, and the last to settle on this land were the first ones here. Things shift, nothing can be taken at face value, and everything always means too much.

This land is awash with memory, driven by memory. And memory, like spite, is bottomless. Nothing is ever forgotten, much less forgiven, and time is a revolving door, where faith runs loops around fact and fact turns into fiction, fiction into history, and history into enduring gall. Between you and everyone else here there is—as Rousseau said of his lifelong, devoted mistress—not the least spark of love.

Politics and religion are so intricately braided that, in talking about the current conflict, it is customary to refer to the Israelis as Jews and to the Palestinians as Arabs. Apples and oranges. We speak of nationalism, but what we are witnessing is the Ayatollization of nationalism—a mix of barbarism, spirituality, and abominable claptrap. It killed Sadat. It killed Rabin. It will kill others.

But there are temperate moments as well. To celebrate the indivisible Muslim-Christian coalition in the new Bethlehem on Christmas Eve, someone suggested releasing inflatable Santas into the night sky. Then they decided to release inflatable Arafats as well. Both ideas were nixed.

A man opens the door to Mayor Freij's conference room and carries in two demitasses. He places one before the mayor, another before me. The mayor is a cordial man, but he is uncomfortable with mannered civilities and assumes I will drink my coffee without being prompted. I remember visiting powerful Egyptians in their offices with my father thirty years ago, and watching him try to negotiate thorny points in the best Arabic he—a foreigner and a Jew—could muster while sipping coffee. I, too, am now drinking coffee with an Arab, discussing, after many years, more or less the same unspoken, unresolved issue: can there be truth, let alone friendship, between Arabs and Jews? The answer, even if it is no, is irrelevant. There will never be real trust between the English and the French either. What matters is not so much peace as willingness to consider peace.

"Process" is a tricky word: it embraces neither the present nor the future tense but something grammarians might call the imperfect conditional. In other words, neither here nor there. Still, people speak of the fruits of the peace process as if something that is neither here nor there could actually bear fruit. Itzhak, who is very lucid, could not have said it more clearly. "I trust the peace process not because I have faith in it but because I have nothing else." Some of the best contracts are forged that way.

Freij, then seventy-seven, the mayor of Bethlehem since 1972, whose political savvy allowed him to survive Jordanian rule, the Israeli occupation, the Intifada, and the ensuing terrorism with surprising agility, says he may seek re-election, though some suspect he covets the ministry of tourism under Arafat. He believes that Bethlehem and the Palestinians have yet to reap the fruits of peace. He complains that the closing of the Israeli borders has had a disastrous and humiliating effect on people who—he points out the window—are right now standing in the rain to obtain entry permits to Israel. The unemployment rate here stands at approximately 40 percent, and yet the mayor claims that with the closing of the border following a wave of terrorist attacks, 80,000 to 100,000 jobs in Israel have gone to Romanian, Thai, Filipino, and Portuguese workers. He understands Israeli fears . . . His sentence trails off.

The mayor turns his attention to the Christmas revels. The date originally proposed for the transfer to Palestinian self-rule was December 25. Christian Palestinians, however, who now constitute a minority of the city's population (they used to be the majority in the 1940s), wanted to hold a Christmas service in an independent Bethlehem. So the Israelis agreed to pull out a week earlier, on December 18. An Italian company has offered, free of charge, to install Christmas lights around Manger Square. The mayor expects the celebrations to be substantial and tourism to boom. "But we need hotels," he laments. He wants to redesign Manger Square to accommodate more buses, tourists, restaurants, and hotels, so that the pilgrims can stay the night and not hurry back to Jerusalem after a two-hour visit.

Christmas is good business here: the town's financial well-being relies almost exclusively on tourism. This may explain why, during the Intifada, the citizens of Bethlehem kept the violence relatively tame so as not to frighten off visitors. "They would put their hands into their pockets as if to pick stones, but what they hurled at the Israeli soldiers was paper napkins," an Arab journalist said.

I inquire about the Christians. I try to avoid direct questions, but I ask Freij about the Christians' future prospects in a Muslim world. Are there any similarities between the endangered Copt minority in Egypt and Bethlehem's Christians? "None whatsoever," he replies. He insists that the Christian community is thriving and faces no threats. "Still, many Christians are leaving," he adds upon reflection, confirming my cabdriver's observation. I know the story well. Christians are nervous. Whether or not Freij decides to run, it is quite possible a Muslim will become the next mayor. This does not worry the Christians as much as the fact that Hamas and Islamic fundamentalist elements will inevitably make life difficult for them as a minority. Bethlehem University, which is partly supported by the Vatican, has been asked to build a place for prayer to accommodate Muslim students. Koranic words have been scribbled on church walls. A few years ago, a graffito in Beit Zahur, nearby, proclaimed, "First the Saturday people, then the Sunday people." To illustrate the extent of Christian fears, a conservative Israeli essayist told me that since the announcement of the redeployment of Israeli soldiers from Palestinian territories, more than 10,000 Palestinians, many of them Christian, have applied for Israeli citizenship.

The writing on the wall is clear. There are Christian mothers who breathe easily once their children are safely abroad. Young Christian couples claim they cannot find adequate housing in Bethlehem and therefore leave. There are numerous Orthodox Palestinian communities in South America. Many Christians apply to emigrate.

I want to ask Freij whether a latter-day Joseph and Mary would come to Bethlehem or whether they would flee to South America instead. I know what he would say.

I am waiting for Moishe, the cabby, on Manger Square. A boy wandering about the square hugs what seems to be a bundle of newspapers but is really a collection of sides of corrugated cardboard boxes.

A man at a pastry stall catches me staring at a huge round rainbow cake. He offers me a slice. I have to accept, though its dubious ingredients trouble me. Someone is scowling in my direction. I feel uneasy. Everyone is glaring. I tell myself I am imagining things.

This place is hardly welcoming. I try to think of the sheep I had seen on the way up to Bethlehem and of Shepherds' Field nearby, and of Bach's "Sheep May Safely Graze." But the melody, so familiar, will not come.

Instead, I hear the voice of the muezzin intone the opening call to prayer from a loudspeaker at the very top of the minaret on

Manger Square. *Allah is great, Allah is great, Allah. There is no Allah but Allah.*

After summoning the faithful to prayer, the muezzin begins a sermon. People are drawn closer together, packing the entrance to the mosque, which is already full. I understand now why young men were thronging along the walls only ten minutes earlier; they were saving the spot nearest the mosque.

The sermon, which I don't understand, is impassioned. The muezzin frequently repeats the words *amrikan, yahud, harb,* meaning Americans, Jews, war, but I don't know the context and don't want to mistake what I fear is being said for what, perhaps, is not being said. Some of the faithful, arriving late, find no room and move across the road, clustering outside the Christmas Tree, where an Israeli Army patrol car has also staked a position. A teenage boy passes in front of those packed by the café and makes the sign of the cross. It is not even clear who is snubbing whom: the Israelis parked three yards away from the Muslims or the Muslims who decide to pray right in front of the army jeep. Everyone is aware of everyone else, the atmosphere is tense and hostile, and everything is being done with an "in your face" attitude. It could not be otherwise in a square that has a steeple, a minaret, and a flagpole that bears the Israeli flag. Rarely in my life have I sensed collective anger seething to the point of explosion. The sermon lasts forty minutes.

And still no Moishe.

Then there is a change of voices and the muezzin intones something I recall from the past and have not heard in thirty years. These are the opening verses of the Koran, and they fill me with a sense of joy and serenity I have not experienced all day. I remember learning these verses long ago in Egypt, and the punishment for not learning them fast enough, and the sense of dread with which I, a Jew, would go up to the front of the class and recite what I feared I had not studied; I never knew at what point, during my recitation, things would break down. But I also remember waking late on winter Fridays and hearing the voice of the muezzin, realizing there was no school that day. And I remember the clear morning sky on summer Fridays when we would head for the beaches, listening to the opening verse reverberate in the Alexandrian sky, still and beautiful, relayed from mosque to mosque, from all corners of the city, until it reached us on the beaches, which were empty because all the men had gone to pray.

Suddenly there is a mad rush into the square. People seem to be coming from everywhere, from the marketplace especially, each carrying a square of corrugated cardboard in his hand. The little boy with the great stack does a brisk business selling them to those who did not bring their own. It is time for prayer, and the faithful begin to prostrate themselves, using the cardboards as makeshift prayer rugs on the streets and sidewalks. Rows of prostrating men form rapidly, each growing in size as stragglers keep joining in. "Allah!" the muezzin sputters, "Allah," he repeats in a heartrending, disconsolate, last gasp of sadness so intense that it hovers over the crowd like a benediction filled with grief, love, and premonition, though no one cries and no one seems moved and everyone thinks only of praying. "Allah," the muezzin intones, with the sorrow of prophets who have stood by and worried for mankind and watched cities die. There is no more stirring sound in the world. "Allah," he repeats, his voice almost crackling with emotion. Then, totally sobered, "May Allah be with you," and finally he closes.

Without any show of emotion, people pick up their cardboard pieces and go back to what they were doing before the prayer.

Gradually, voices and shouts can be heard rising in the market-place. Things are back to normal. I hear the words *kheyar, zeitoun,* and *marameyeh*—cucumbers, olives, and sage. I have not heard them in thirty years. The last time I walked into a souk must have been with my mother, when I was ten.

Later that day, I am standing high on the Mount of Olives in East Jerusalem with Itzhak. The clouds have broken momentarily and we are standing along the parapet looking over a sunlit view of the Old City, studded with beautiful olive groves. Olive trees are not beautiful and yet they are—stumpy, majestic, austere. I have an impulse to walk down the slope and tear a twig and, as in Dante, watch the tree bleed.

A boy walks up to me and tries to sell me olive leaves. I want to buy the whole branch. But I remember that I have no change and apologize to the boy. He insists I take it anyway. Itzhak says he has some change in the car, opens the door, searches in the glove com-partment, and hands the boy a coin. The boy seems pleased. Itzhak, who knows how to leave you alone, probably suspects I am thinking of peace symbols. But I am thinking of Jesus on Gethse-mane looking down over Jerusalem, his sweat falling like drops of blood, sensing that someone is about to betray him.

So this is where He was born, I think, scanning the horizon for Bethlehem. I want to nurse this thought, to stroke its beauty and feel what I know I will never have words for. But suddenly a tussle breaks out between the boy who sold me the olive branch and another boy who is trying to sell palm fronds. The olive boy kicks the palm boy. I turn and am about to tell them to stop, but Itzhak is faster than I am and yells at them in Hebrew. The boys pay no heed and are now throwing punches at each other. Itzhak urges two Arabs sitting on the wall to do something to stop the fight. But the men do not budge, do not seem interested, and go on talking. Now Itzhak gets in between the boys and separates them, pushing each away, cursing in Arabic, still imploring the men to help. One of the boys begins to cry: I know how these things can turn. All we need is an Israeli grabbing an Arab boy. "Let's go," I tell Itzhak. He is breathing hard, obviously more disturbed than I thought. Meanwhile, a camel, with its rider, squats on the ground not far from us and urinates. The stench is unbearable and the stream endless. "Yes, let's go," Itzhak says.

As we drive down the slope, I turn to take a last look at the Mount of Olives, thinking of Bethlehem and the broadcast of Midnight Mass that I know I, too, will be listening for this year. Itzhak chuckles. He has heard a rumor that the Israelis may be asked to help with the broadcast. The Palestinians want to be in charge of transmitting the Midnight Mass from the Church of St. Catherine, but they don't have the expertise. So they will ask the Jews to help a predominantly Muslim city broadcast a Christian Mass.

"And we'll do it," Itzhak adds. "It's Christmas."

Becket's Winter

⁂

For about a month or so in the winter of 1965, we spoke of little else but the movie *Becket*. *Becket* burst into our narrow little world the way all great dramas do when they suddenly take over a community, stirring new fantasies, latching on to old ones, giving our thoughts an edge and a wisdom we never knew we had, working its way deep into every crevice of our subconscious until we were no longer able to remember who or what we were before the play. I call it *Becket*'s winter, the way Shakespeare's contemporaries might have called the 1600–1601 season the year of *Hamlet*, for after seeing *Hamlet* everyone is changed. *Becket* has become a marker, one of those time posts around which we situate events we would otherwise forget or lose track of. The play remembers them for us; over time, 1965, that ugly year that brought such terrible changes in our lives, has become a pale, lusterless satellite which periodically strays into the reflected light of the movie.

We had terrible worries that winter, and there were always rumors that the police would come to search our home or take my father away. And yet I doubt that I would have remembered these incidents as vividly as I do today had *Becket* not been laced into them. Not a day went by that winter without someone speaking of *Becket* or of the police. We spoke of *Becket* to forget the police, to forget the anonymous calls every night, to forget that we were among the last Jews of Alexandria. Perhaps we spoke of *Becket* because there was nothing else to speak about, because, in the end, all that was left in our culture-starved world was—movies. Movies held great sway in Alexandria, displacing everything, including our worst fears. Movies screened those fears. And yet it is thanks to that screen today that I remember our fears.

Everyone fell under their spell. My father, who had lost his business and had no notion what or where to turn to next; my mother, who was deaf and did not wish to face the truth about our abysmal prospects in Egypt; I, who always had my nose in books—or, as my grandmother said, my head in the clouds—down to my grandmother, a practical woman in her nineties whose feet were firmly planted not only on the ground but, as I liked to say, under it as well—all of us gave way to *Becket*. Even our cook, who, tired of hearing so much about the movie, decided to go one evening and, for the equivalent of about seven cents, had his fill of Jean Anouilh's *Becket*, courtesy of Arabic subtitles. He, too, had caught the bug.

The only one who resisted was my great-aunt, who was almost blind and never went to the movies and who, for entertainment, would listen to quiz shows on Radio Monte Carlo. She was a religious woman and perhaps did not like all this talk of church in a Jewish home.

Otherwise *Becket* was everywhere. Not a single magazine failed to mention it. *Becket* came into all my classes: in English class, where we were studying Chaucer's prologue, in history class, where our teacher taught an already obsessed class all there was to know about excommunication; even the choir of the American Mission School, under the expert direction of a native-born Alexandrian, was glad to oblige with a few Gregorian chants, enough to stem the irreversible tide of Beatlemania which had already seized Alexandria by storm the previous year. And finally, *Becket* won over our group at school, where, no matter what part we played, all we wanted was to capture the sinister grin and the nasal ironies of Richard Burton, or the hysterical bawling of Peter O'Toole. Some of us wrote papers on Emperor Henry IV of Germany, whose famous three-day, barefooted stand at snowbound Canossa in 1077 finally moved Pope Gregory VII to revoke his excommunication ban. The first piece I read by an unheard-of poet called T. S. Eliot was *Murder in the Cathedral*. Without it, I might have gone years more without knowing *Four Quartets*, or *The Waste Land*, or "The Lovesong of J. Alfred Prufrock."

Medieval England was everywhere, even if the Egypt of the mid-sixties was Egypt at its most anti-English. It never occurred to us that this play which seemed so prototypically British could have been written by a Frenchman. I read it in English, though French is my mother tongue, siding with the British against the French, though, in reading *Henry V*, I'd always rooted for the French against the British at Agincourt.

For a whole week, at the age of fourteen, all I did every evening was ride the tramway to the main station in Alexandria, buy about ten loose cigarettes, purchase my ticket at the Cinema Strand, and enter this dark world to which I had arrived purposely late so as to miss the previews, the newsreel, and the cartoons. I knew most of the lines by heart; I still do now, thirty years later. This, I think, is what people mean by the magic of the stage or of the silver screen. It consumes you as you're watching, haunts you as you leave, and never lets go, that night, or the next, or the one after that. It became a compulsion to return every evening at the same time to the same seat to the same show, a compulsion which, like all addictions—to gambling, drugs, alcohol, or pleasure—corrupts us not because it excludes even those we love but because it allows us to devote ourselves entirely to ourselves, to our pleasure. I, too, like King Henry II—or like King Philip II in *Don Carlos*—was learning how to be alone. In this, I had found a sister soul. My sympathies were always with the lonely King, never with Becket, or the honor of God.

I shall never forget the opening scene: the Gregorian chant immediately following the credits, the lofty view from the cathedral's large belfry, the King dismounting and then entering a dark nave and finally kneeling before his old friend Becket's tomb, asking with almost rakish melancholy, "Well, Thomas Becket, are you satisfied?"

Then I know the journey has started. It is the story of an impossible friendship between two men, one who loves, or says he loves; the other who doesn't, or says he can't. One tyrannizes but is always rebuffed; the other gives but never yields. The ill-tempered King with soulful urges, and the high-minded Archbishop who is at once cunning and sincere in a world where "sincerity [has become] a form of strategy." Everyone changes—or, rather, molts his older self. The erstwhile dissolute playboy turns into an earnest priest, and the anti-clerical monarch ends lonelier than a monk in an empty palace. As in all good stories, the cat's cradle goes on forever.

Between the two giants are the jealous barons, the chiding mother, sniveling heirs, and the snarling young Queen, the famous Eleanor of Aquitaine, whose "carping mediocrity" is matched only by her body—that "empty desert which duty forced [the King] to wander in alone"! Everyone envies Henry's love for Becket. Finally, the sparring comic duo, the Pope and the Cardinal, double- and triple-dealing with each other, two foxes outfoxing each other at the nth remove, while they bilk both Becket and Henry, almost without thinking.

Becket: the man whose talents were for sale to the highest bidder until God outbid them all; the jack-of-all-trades who "improvises his honor" and collaborates with the enemy, but is neither a Norman nor really just Saxon any longer. Towering over everyone at court, he thinks and knows too much; he is elusive with others and himself, distrusts everyone, but most of all himself, especially after his conversion. Becket, the man who found nothing truly worthy of love until a capricious ploy verging on a royal prank steers him to the righteous path: against Becket's wish, the King laughingly appoints him Archbishop of Canterbury. But as in the legend of Saint Genesius, the man who thought he was only playing the part of the holy man becomes a holy man indeed. The vocation is almost thrust on him, it comes too easily, and in good Augustinian fashion, Becket is wary of saintliness itself, for saintliness—as both he and his rival Gilbert Folliot know—is a temptation, too, "one of the [devil's] most insidious and fearsome snares."

Then there's the King: as ill-mannered, vindictive, and guileless as a spoiled brat who was never taught to be alone and who, like a snubbed lover now, must learn to deal with loss as he bawls and aches, seeking comfort, but finding pity instead. He exacts revenge and he gets it. But he won't commit the deed himself. "Will no one rid me of him?" and "Are there none but cowards like myself around me?" he asks. A coward needs others to do his dirty work. But he needs others to blame as well.

The symmetries here are almost too ironic. Becket, who helped foil an assassination attempt on the King while visiting a cathedral in France, is himself downed by the King's four barons in his own cathedral. But the King, who thought he could outsmart his old friend, is caught in the snare as well. To appease the Saxon population, which has seen its beloved Archbishop murdered by Norman henchmen, the King must now kneel on exactly the same spot where his friend had breathed his last, and there be flogged by no less than four monks. Tit for tat. "Are you satisfied now, Becket?" asks the King as he prepares to stand up and forgive the four monks who administered the lashes. "Does this settle our account?" After which, the King puts on his shirt and swears to one of his baffled barons that the law will have to seek out those guilty of the murder.

No parody of justice has ever been more wicked.

The King, one senses, has lost everything he cared for and is now condemned to wander the icy, wintry palace rooms, learning, as he says, "to be alone again."

One is not always left alone in life. But at some point or other, one will eventually be alone again. It's the *again* that smarts. For it tells us that some things in life never change; they may go away for a while, but loneliness, the one we know so well and thought we had finally overcome, always comes back in the end.

I have heard Peter O'Toole say these words at least thirty times in my life. I do not remember each one, but I know that each viewing is indissolubly fused with the others, that each time I hear these words I have not only aged and added an annual ring to a heap of memories, but that with these words my youth, my past, Alexandria, those who have died, and those other parts of me that are probably dead are summarily evoked: the boy who went to see *Becket* with his parents the first time, then with his friends, and then for an entire, unforgettable week by himself, always trying to recapture the miracle of the first viewing, not just in Alexandria, but immediately after we left, in Italy, where I saw the film dubbed in Italian, and then in France, in England, and for so many years afterward on television in the States, in college, graduate school, trying to recapture the dour sense of foreboding and of unspoken warning laced in the King's message to the young man I was then that I, too, one day would have to learn to be alone again, that in the end the work of memory is the work of loneliness.

The last time I saw *Becket* in Egypt was on a Sunday evening a week before we left. That afternoon I had taken my grandmother and my great-aunt to their club, where they said their goodbyes to their old friends. When we returned home, we were greeted by the strong smell of leather from all our packed suitcases, which were neatly stacked throughout the house. No one was home.

Once I was inside, my impulse was always to turn on the lights in the entry and rush down the dark, oppressive corridor to light up one room after the other: the pantry, the kitchen, the small living room, most of the bedrooms, hoping to rouse the entire house and give myself and the elderly sisters who stood disheartened in the foyer the illusion that others were in the house as well but were not quite ready to come out of their rooms, though they were pleased to hear our voices and would presently show their faces.

But even the lights did not help. Under my great-aunt's thrifty management of household finances all the bulbs had been replaced with ones of such inferior wattage that my mother was tempted to compare the once-resplendent living-room chandelier to a dying man's bedside lamp.

I opened the window to let in the city noise. It came, though distant and untouched, like the laughter of passersby who don't know someone is dying upstairs. This lifeless, gloomy cloud would not disperse. The only way to shake it off was either to go out again, or see a movie, or read a book. The large radio had already been disassembled and packed in a large crate and was sitting somewhere on the docks. There was nothing to do. "It feels like a medieval crypt in here," said my great-aunt. My grandmother shot me a quizzical glance; neither of us knew what had brought this on. It wasn't like her to complain of the gloom.

After tea, my grandmother took out the needlepoint she had started two years earlier, a reduced replica of a kilim in the living room. My great-aunt, who had stopped reading altogether because of her eyes, had asked me to read aloud a novel in Italian.

After a short while, my grandmother removed her eyeglasses and rubbed her eyes, saying her eyes, too, were tired. Then she put the glasses back on again. Her sister wasn't listening to my reading. She, too, removed her glasses and looked tired, bored.

"What was the name of that movie you were talking about the other day?" asked my great-aunt.

"Which movie?" I asked, knowing exactly which film she meant yet determined not to give in to her squeamish reluctance to come straight to the point and name contemporary works by their proper names.

"You know, the one about the English king who appoints an archbishop who then turns against him."

I made as though I still did not understand.

"*Becket*," I answered dryly in the end.

"Ah yes, *Becket*." A moment of silence elapsed. "*Becket?*" she seemed to ask as though puzzled by the word.

"Look, he already told you it's *Becket*," interjected my grandmother, "and *Becket* it is! Why do you ask all these questions?"

"It was just that I was thinking, maybe, one day, we could go to the movies instead of staying all cooped up here like troglodytes."

"To the movies?" wondered my grandmother, equally determined to make things difficult for her sister.

"I didn't say we *had* to go to the movies. It was just a thought. Never mind. Movies are bad for my eyes anyway."

"Do you want to go, yes or no?" asked my grandmother.

Her sister hesitated. "If everyone else wants to, then, why not? It wouldn't be so terrible."

"If we want to go to the movies, we have to leave right away," said my grandmother.

"Why, is it far?" she asked.

"It's playing at the Strand," I said.

"But that's only a tram ride away," she exclaimed, as though startled by the revelation. "It would be all right, wouldn't it?"

"It's fine, it's fine," grumbled my grandmother, finally lodging her needle in the canvas and putting the canvas away. "All this palaver to say let's go to the movies."

We rushed to the station. A tram came soon enough, and luckily, we found three seats together. As usual, the sisters bickered as to who would sit next to the window to shield the other from the draft, which cut like a blade, they said. Toward the end of the trip, my grandmother searched through her purse and gave me a five-pound note. Being a man, I was to pay for all three of us.

The lobby was already empty, and it occurred to me that there might be no seats left. I was wrong.

From behind a very thick curtain one could already hear a month-old American newsreel. The cartoons would come next. Then the previews. I led the two old ladies into the theater. Then the usher helped me escort them in the dark. It took us a while until they removed their coats and sat down. When we were seated, my grandmother held my hand.

During intermission, I brought three ices. A young Austrian couple, sitting across the aisle, came to greet us. I was busy unwrapping my cone and failed to stand up.

The sisters would not stop reprimanding me for my rudeness during our ride home by cab. I had almost ruined *Becket* for them, not standing up in front of Monsieur and Madame Horkheimer! "Plus," added Grandmother, "I wish you would stop wearing these long blue trousers with copper snaps all over them."

"What snaps?" I asked.

"The pants that cowboys wear."

I did not answer. But a thought flared through my mind. I would pretend to get very annoyed with them, lose my temper, stop the cab, and walk back to the Strand and catch the nine o'clock show. A moment later, I heard myself asking the driver to let me out. I was going to walk home, I said.

"But don't you have homework?" asked both sisters, who probably didn't want to be left alone that evening. I didn't answer. I shut the door of the cab and watched the car speed ahead.

Alone on the road that Sunday evening, I found my heart racing at the merest thought of going to a late-late show by myself for the first time. All the store lights were out, and up ahead, past the dark in the direction of the movie theater, I could make out two Greek cafés glowing in their yellow haze. If I could go to the nine o'clock show by myself, then other things were possible, too, I thought, as I lit a cigarette, roused by so much freedom earned with such great ease, realizing for the first time in all these weeks that, despite my love for the movie, *Becket* may have been an elaborate and wonderful excuse for staying out alone past midnight. I'd see *Becket* a second time tonight. Bold thoughts rushed through my mind and thrilled me beyond anything I had known in my life.

As I headed toward the crowd, I began to hear something behind me. I pretended to ignore it and continued to walk. It came closer. "Where are you headed all by yourself at this time?" asked a voice. I let a few seconds pass. Finally I turned around. It was my grandmother. She had rolled down the windows of the cab and was begging me to come in. I hesitated awhile, struggling not to tell her to go home and leave me alone. Then there was a pause, the cab stopped, and the door opened. "Come on," she said. "Don't be angry."

Before I knew it, I had stepped into the car and taken my usual seat between the old ladies, feeling very much like a hapless King Henry surrendering once again to two chiding women whose meddling claims could snuffle the light of love, of joy, and desire, but who, in so doing, had also spared me from something unknown and dangerous which continued to thrill me, if only because it frightened me more than the shame of cowardice, more than regret, more than yielding and going home with two old ladies to be alone again. "There will be other times," they said.

There never were. I never saw *Becket* again in Alexandria.

I was grateful, but I never forgave them.

I am still owed that one night. And when I go to see *Becket* now, I do so not only to remember someone whose desire continues to haunt an empty sidewalk after many years, but to expiate an old wish, the way we go back to lost opportunities and airy might-have-beens, knowing that old scores can never be settled, that what is gone is lost indeed, that the play I see each time is a new play, not the play I never saw that night, that all we have in the end is ourself, our loneliness—not even our memories but how they've lied to us, not *Becket* but what we've done with it.

In a Double Exile

❊

There comes the time at every Passover Seder when someone opens a door to let in the prophet Elijah. At that moment, something like a spell invariably descends over the celebrants, and everyone stares at the doorway, trying to make out the quiet movements of the prophet as he glides his way in and takes the empty seat among us.

But by then my mind has already drifted many, many times, and like all disbelievers who find themselves wondering why they are attending a Seder after last year's resolution, I begin to think of how little this ritual means to me—recalling the ten plagues, the crossing of the Red Sea, manna from heaven. All of it keenly arranged to let every kind of Jew find something to celebrate.

For the religious, Passover is the grateful remembrance of a homeward journey after years of suffering.

For those who believe in the spirit more than in the letter of the occasion, the holiday celebrates survival and deliverance from all forms of tyranny—survival after Auschwitz, freedom from anti-Semitism in Russia, Ethiopia, and Syria.

For yet others, Passover is an occasion to gather around a table and link arms with Jews from everywhere and all times.

I don't know Hebrew. Nor do I know any of the songs or prayers. I can't even tell when the Seder is officially over. Often I suspect the whole ceremony has petered out or has been cut short for my benefit—or been drawn out to prove a point. I always attend with misgivings, which I communicate to others at the table, and try to atone for by reading aloud when my turn comes, only to resent having been asked to read.

And as I sit and stew, feeling ever more trapped among the observant, I too begin to think of Egypt, of this Egypt everyone will invoke at sundown tomorrow night and which symbolizes suffering, exile, and captivity, and suddenly appears in our dining room like a mummy whose sleep has been disturbed: unreal, mythic, faraway Egypt, which everyone calls by its Hebrew name, *Mizrayim*; in Arabic, it is *Misr*. The same words, but eons apart.

Then, as happens every year, I begin to think of another Egypt, the one I was born in and knew and got to love and would never have left had not a modern pharaoh named Gamal Abdel Nasser forced me out for being Jewish. This was an Egypt many of us would have stayed in, even as the last Jews of the land, which we nearly were, even if we had had to beg to stay, which indeed we did.

Often in those years in Alexandria, when I was growing up, Passover coincided with Easter and Ramadan. During Ramadan, we would be let out of school at about noon every day, because Muslims, who fasted all day, needed to rest in the afternoon before breaking their fast at sunset.

To those of us who did not have to nap, these were the most magical hours of the year. The city was always quiet then, there was hardly any homework, and summer was only a few weeks away.

At the Seder, the men in my family would spar, my father begging my uncle to speed it up, my uncle deferring to tradition instead, everyone more or less giggling, including the one or two Christians visiting that evening who were hauled in to a dinner that reminded them so much of the Last Supper, they said, everyone garbling everything in a blithe chorus of *"Next year in Jerusalem,"* until we heard the cannon of Ramadan announce it was time for devout Muslims to eat.

It never occurred to us that a Seder in Egypt was a contradiction in terms.

Now, when everyone speaks of Pharaoh at Passover, I think back to my very last Seder in Egypt, on the eve of our departure for Italy in 1965—a long, mirthless, desultory affair, celebrated with weak lights and all the shutters drawn so that no one in the street might suspect what we were up to that night.

After almost three centuries of religious tolerance, we found ourselves celebrating Passover the way our Marrano ancestors had done under the Spanish Inquisition: in secret, verging on shame, without conviction, in great haste, and certainly without a clear notion of what we were celebrating. Was it the first exodus from Egypt? Or maybe the second from Spain? Or the third from Turkey? Or the fourth, when my family members fled Italy just before the Nazis took over? Or were we celebrating the many exoduses that went unrecorded but that every Jew knows he can remember if he tries hard enough, for each one of us is a dislodged citizen of a country that was never really his but that he has learned to long for and cannot forget. The fault lines of exile and diaspora always run deep, and we are always from elsewhere, and from elsewhere before that.

Everything in history happens twice, wrote Marx, the first time as tragedy, the second as farce. He forgot to add that Jewish history is repetition, the history of repetition.

Caught in these loops and coils, my family forgot to remember the obvious—that Egypt was never our home, that we should never have come back after Moses, that we didn't even know where our home was, much less which language was ours. We had borrowed everyone else's. Some of us forgot we were Jews. Alexandria was our mirage—in the desert, we dreamed awhile longer.

In the end, Egyptian nationalism drove us all away. Today, religious intolerance wants to finish the job for everyone who remains, not just Jews. Copts—Christians who are thought to be among the most direct descendants of the ancient Egyptians—and Westernized Egyptians are watching the clouds darken around the country. Will Egypt drown again? In 1981, the assassination of President Anwar el-Sadat, in recent years the killings of tourists and Egyptian intellectuals, and in October 1995 the stabbing of the writer and Nobel laureate Naguib Mahfouz—are these the new plagues? Must I worry and remember for Egypt as well now?

Passover is the night for it. For on that night all Jews remember the night when Jewish memory began. That night each one of us thinks back to that private Egypt we each carry with us wherever we are. We may not always know what to remember, but we know we must remember.

In my case, I remember a city called Alexandria, a city as remote to me now as Egypt is to my American friends who will celebrate Passover, a city that was never mine, that no longer exists as I knew it, but that rushes into the room each time they open the door for Elijah to remind me that I will never say, Next year in Jerusalem, in Alexandria again.

A Late Lunch

※

My father comes fifteen minutes early. I arrive forty minutes late.
He says he doesn't mind waiting. He always has something to read.
I can see him sitting quietly behind the large window inside the
Museum of Modern Art's lobby, seemingly unaware of the crowd of
tourists milling around the gift shop and the information desk. I
rush out of the taxicab with my five-year-old son, Alex. It's raining.
I'll blame the rain, I think.

We're barely in time for a late lunch. We wait in line at the cafe-
teria and decide to share the same tray. My father likes the chili
here; I order some, too; Alex doesn't know what he wants, so we
pick up a fruit platter and a handful of bread sticks. We argue over
who is to pay. My father relents and offers to find a table while I
wait in the cashier's line. He reminds me not to forget his coffee. I
nod and watch his small figure dart into the dining hall. He stops,
scans the crowd once more, then scurries toward an empty table by
the window at the far corner and proceeds to lay our raincoats
down on the chairs.

He is pleased with himself. Our corner overlooks the gleaming wet patio, which on rainy days always reminds me of Alexandria. The storm patters on the large glass pane. It feels snug inside. I look at him again and know he has thought of Alexandria, too.

And as I watch him slowly scoop up the first spoonful of chili, followed by a piece of bread, which he always butters with the scrupulous devotion of men who know the good things in life, I catch a fugitive look on his face that seems to ask, "What's the matter, why aren't you eating?" I shrug, as if alleging a stray thought. I look down at my food and look up again, realizing that I, too, am happy today—happy to be with him, to see him with my son, to know, as I catch him avoiding my eyes, that what matters to me now is not his love but his willingness to be loved, to come because I called.

We're interrupted by the apparition of two women advancing slowly to a table nearby. He stares at them. "I like to come here . . ." he begins. I am reminded of how thoroughly and desperately he likes women! "There are days when every woman is beautiful," he says, as though speaking of fruits that ripen everywhere on the same day. I know he wants to talk about women. As always, I steer the conversation away and ask about my mother instead. "What's there to say?" he replies. "Your mother . . ."

I am about to deflect this as well, when it dawns on me that perhaps our improvised lunch is nothing more than an uncomfortably staged affair between a father eager to say a few things to his son and a son who doesn't want to regret one day having failed to let him say them.

I take a first, shy, tentative step and ask, "Why did you ever marry her?"

"Whoever remembers?" he replies. Why did he have children? "Because I had to."

But who ordered you? "No one," he says, "it was just to make her happy."

He looks around again. "All I wanted was to read books," he adds. "On the second night of our honeymoon, while she slept, I opened the balcony door, and staring at the beachfront facing our hotel, I knew it was wrong. I wanted to study Greek, I wanted to write and travel and be free to love as I pleased. I wanted to leave our bedroom and go downstairs and keep walking past the empty garden and go away, but I didn't dare." Silence. "I forced myself to love her," he says. "Then one day it was over. Or at least someone else made me see it was over."

There is a strained pause in our conversation.

"Who?" I ask.

"You know who," he says without hesitating, almost grateful I had made it easy for him.

He calls her *That one*. I say nothing and, instead, play the open-minded, freethinking grown-up who knows how to listen to such tales.

"She still calls me."

This I can't believe. More than thirty years later?

"In the middle of the night, when it's daylight over there, she calls."

"And what does Mother say?"

He shrugs.

I can just see him tiptoeing into the living room at three in the morning, tying his bathrobe, whispering in the dark to a woman halfway across the world and at the other end of time, who is probably irritated he's mumbling and can't speak any louder on the phone.

"She has a grown-up daughter. She misses me, she says. She thinks I'm still forty-five; I tell her I'm almost twice that. She doesn't understand, she wants to come, she wants a picture of me."

He stares at me, as if to ask, Can you figure women out?

And suddenly I find myself saying something that is more shocking to me than news of the woman's existence.

"Instead of pictures, why don't you just go back for a few weeks. I'll take care of the rest." By the rest I mean my mother.

"But I've grown old, I'm a grandfather." He turns to my son. "Besides, she says she's fat now."

"Just go," I say, mocking his feigned reluctance.

My father sits quietly. There is no more coffee in his cup; he says he will get some for me as well.

"Everyone is allowed five good years in their life. I've had my five. Everyone meets a dangerous woman in his life. I've met mine."

"Go to Egypt," I interrupt without even looking at him.

"I need more coffee," he says, standing up. "Anyway, first find me a decent picture and then we'll see." He throws a hand in the air to mean he doesn't care, that he's far too old for this, that the whole idea is one big nuisance.

The dining room is almost empty now, and as I watch him head for the coffee machine and disappear into the serving area, I am thinking of the years ahead when I'll come here alone, or with my son, and remember this one day when we sat together as if posing for a mental photograph, thinking of Alexandria, listening to this cheerless tale of two lovers cast adrift in time. We'll sit at this very table and wait for him, and think he's only gone for coffee and is coming back shortly, carrying two fresh cups and dessert on a tray as he did that day when he returned to the table and asked almost casually: "By the way, do you happen to have a picture of me? I mean, a good one?"

Underground

❖

Whenever the Seventh Avenue train races between Eighty-sixth and Ninety-sixth Streets and offers a fleeting, darkened glimpse of what looks like latter-day catacombs, the question invariably arises: What is it? From the windows of the Broadway Local the ghost of this Stone Age grotto, suddenly illumined by the speeding train, is a place only Dante or Kafka might have imagined. The walls are begrimed with thick 1970s-style graffiti, while something resembling a platform, strewn with debris, stands in the ashen dimness of places most cities would rather forget about.

But we stare all the same, until springing into view like painted letters on the hull of a sunken liner are the telltale faded mosaics spelling a station's name: Ninety-first Street. The name appears again on a higher panel, framed by terra-cotta molding with golden numerals in relief, a combination typical of the cartouche created by Heins & LaFarge, the firm originally commissioned to design subway ceramics.

I became intrigued by the Ninety-first Street Station while riding the Broadway Local during one of its arbitrary halts. The train idled to a halt outside Ninety-first, and during my enforced wait, I became aware of, then curious about, this abandoned stop. On my first extended view of the place, I was most struck by what was absent: no old-fashioned wooden token booth, no benches. The benches, says Joe Cunningham, a transportation and engineering historian, were removed as fire hazards, while turnstiles, originally installed in the early twenties, were salvaged for parts. There were no print ads along the walls. A sealed bathroom door was slightly discernible behind a loud smear of graffiti.

Of course, there couldn't be an outlet to the street, though a shaft of light seemed to beam along the skeletal treads of a stairway. At the tail end of the station, a barely perceptible, differently styled ceramic tile suggested that however short its life span, even this station had gone through a face-lift and bore the traces of its various incarnations.

Similar alterations are hardly unusual in New York's subways or in the city itself, where everything is a patchwork of swatches and layers, of bits and pieces, slapped together until you cannot see the fault lines for the surface, nor the surface for the patchwork. Subway corridors, stairwells, and sidewalk entrances are known to have disappeared, and tiled alcoves, designed to accommodate vintage phone booths, have vanished behind newly erected walls that sprout doors to become makeshift toolsheds. Ancient men's rest rooms, famed for their shady practices, have mended their ways and been converted into candy stands.

Nothing is ever really demolished or dismantled down below, but everything is tentative and amorphous. From the width of platforms to the shape of lamp sockets down to the form of pillars (round, square, steel-beam), everything changes in the space of a few yards and betrays the many ways in which the city has always had to adjust to shifting demographics.

Stations whose token booths are absurdly positioned at the extreme end of the platform—Seventy-ninth, Eighty-sixth, and 110th Streets on Broadway, for example—will have their madness forgiven once you are told that they were designed to accommodate trains far shorter than those of today. It was because the Eighty-sixth and Ninety-sixth Street platforms were extended to twice their size to receive ten-car trains that the Ninety-first Street Station, caught between the two and nearly touching both, saw the writing on the wall. It became obsolete. Its time, like that of the Eighteenth Street Station on the East Side or of the Worth Street and City Hall Stations, had run out. On February 2, 1959, the Ninety-first Street Station was closed permanently.

When asked, middle-aged New Yorkers seldom recall even missing the station. Like a friend who died and whose name mysteriously disappears from the Manhattan telephone book, the Ninety-first Street Station no longer exists on any of the Metropolitan Transportation Authority's maps. It is extinct. Or is it, perhaps, just vestigial?

Indeed, the question I ask when passing the Ninety-first Street Station is not simply *What is it?* or *What happened here?* but something more wistful and unwieldy: *What if?* What if, instead of having the train dawdle awhile between stations, the conductor stopped at Ninety-first Street and on a mad impulse announced the station's name, and then, carried away by the sound of his own words, forgot himself and suddenly opened the doors and began discharging passengers? Some of them would actually walk out, half startled and dazed, heading for imaginary turnstiles, past the old token booth, clambering up the stairway onto a sidewalk awash in the early-evening light as passengers had done for six decades until that fateful day forty years ago.

What if, for a split second, the mid-fifties were suddenly to rush in, the way the thought of them invariably takes hold whenever I think of using not the side entrance to a prewar building on Riverside Drive but the defunct main gate on the drive itself, a gate no one uses any longer, but that, being sealed, beckons like a portal to vanished times?

And what if awaiting me barely a block away is the New Yorker Theater at Eighty-ninth Street, and farther up, the Riviera and the Riverside at Ninety-sixth Street? What if the films they're about to show this year are *Black Orpheus, Room at the Top, North by Northwest, The 400 Blows*, and other late-fifties classics? What if things didn't always have to disappear? What if time took another track, as subways do when there's work ahead? Not backward, just different: a track we can't quite fathom and whose secret conduits linking up the new with the old and the very, very old are known only to the loud yellow repair train that appears from nowhere in the dead of night and then lumbers away like a demoted god.

What if, in spite of its dead silence now, this station were a gateway to an underground that is ultimately less in the city than in ourselves, and that what we see in it is what we dare not see in ourselves? What if, for all its beguiling presence, the Ninety-first Street Station is really not even about time, or about hating to see things go, or about watching places grow more lonely and dysfunctional over time? Instead, what if this underground cavern were my double, a metaphor for the pulsating, dirty, frightened dungeon within all of us which feels as lonely and abandoned, and as out of place and out of sync with the rest of the world, as we all fear we are, though we try to hide it, eager as we are to patch up our uneasiness as fast as we can, hoping that, as fast as it can, too, our train will pass this station by, put it behind us, and take us, like people who have been to see Hades, back to the world of the living?

I finally went to visit the old station one day with a small group of subway aficionados led by Mr. Cunningham on a tour run by the New York Transit Museum at Boerum Place and Schermerhorn Street in downtown Brooklyn. We got on at Ninety-sixth Street and rode in the first car of the Broadway Local. At Ninety-first the train did in fact stop, just as I had fantasized. The conductor opened the front doors only, and to the baffled gaze of the other passengers, we stepped out. Then the doors closed again, and the train left, everyone watching us as though we were spectral travelers headed into a time warp. Wandering through this modern underworld, I tried to think of the great poets and the caves of Lascaux and *Planet of the Apes*, but all I could focus on as I negotiated my way through a thick mantle of soot was dirt, rats, and a faint queasiness.

The platform was filled with trash: broken beams, old cardboard, and a litter of foam cups. This wasn't just the detritus of a subway station but the leftovers of mole people. There was enough of it to confuse future archaeologists, whose job, it suddenly occurred to me, is not only to dig up the past but also to scrape the rubble of squatters from that of the great civilizations whose abandoned homes squatters made their own.

I stood there, staring at what must surely have once been the gleaming tiles of a perfectly proportioned station with its perfectly curved platform. Like all armchair archaeologists, I had come here to prod the raw cells of the city's past and see how everything, down to an unused subway station, can be touched by time and, like the layers underneath the city of Troy, is ultimately sanctified by time.

I wanted to see how inanimate objects refuse to forget or suggest that all cities—like people, like palimpsests, like the remains of a Roman temple hidden beneath an ancient church—do not simply have to watch themselves go but strive to remember, because in the wish to remember lies the wish to restore, to stay alive, to continue to be.

I knew I would never come here again. But I also knew that I had not put this station behind me either. In a few days I would pass by again and, again as if I'd never stopped here at all or had bungled an experiment I now needed to repeat, would ask myself, again and again, the one question I've been asking each time I speed by Ninety-first on the Broadway Local line and am invariably brought to think of the past: What if the train were to stop one day and let me off?

A Celestial Omnibus

>|<

As it approaches West Seventy-second Street on its way uptown, the M5 bus crosses lanes and begins to bear left on Broadway, hesitating by the old subway house, where it stands and shifts awhile in the shadow of the Ansonia like someone waiting in the cold. Then, with a sudden, jittery swoop, it takes a sharp left turn and enters what will always remain, despite the crowd, the traffic, and drab, faded storefronts, a beguiling kingdom where, enchanted by twilit snow, ordinary city life turns solemn and almost magical.

This is the moment everyone has been waiting for since riding up the Avenue of the Americas and turning left on Fifty-seventh Street; and this is probably why the route was originally conceived years ago. For after turning and picking up more passengers on Seventy-second Street, the bus is suddenly buoyed, as though freed of all cares, shedding the grumpy, snub-nosed character it assumes to get by in the city, while those aboard want to burrow into snug little corners, sip something hot, and, having opened the window just a crack to let in the snowflakes, sit back, relax, and enjoy the ride, as the bus picks up more and more speed, steered by spell-bound hands.

This route lasts for forty-four blocks, from Seventy-second Street to 116th Street, where, after its moment of glory, the bus finally turns right and goes up Claremont Avenue, like a frog who has had his few minutes as a prince and must now jump back into the pond.

But while it lasts, for about twenty minutes or so, you are totally elsewhere, as though headed to the countryside late on a snowy Friday afternoon. And you begin to feel warm and safe, as the bus wends its sinuous course up Riverside Drive, which is lined by buildings on one side and overlooks Riverside Park on the other. Beyond this narrow strip of a park, built by the public works program during the Depression years, is the West Side Highway, which runs the entire length of western Manhattan along the Hudson River. The magic occurs not during the day, nor at night, but at dusk, perhaps because this is when I first took the M5 more than fifteen years ago, by mistake, as these things always happen.

Riding a bus I thought might take me up Broadway but never did, at each successive stop I kept wondering whether to get off, only to find myself postponing my exit every time, mesmerized as I and everyone else was by the oblique sweep of snow racing past the bus windowpanes and, right behind the snow, a stark-lit park from where one could make out mournful slabs of ice inching their way down the Hudson like a flock of lost sheep.

From the other side of the bus, however, a swerving magnificence of concave and convex prewar buildings dutifully follows the contour of the Drive at dusk, coming into view and then receding, allowing the landscape to conjure by turns the country, then the city, only to suggest that perhaps this is really neither the city nor the countryside but an unusual small town that could just as easily have been called St.-Rémy or Bedford Falls. I was, it seemed, not in a bus at all but in a late-nineteenth-century train that would any moment now stop at a snowed-in station where, in the old stationmaster's hut, I was sure to find Frank Capra's pharmacist and van Gogh's postman warming their hands over a cup of red mulled wine.

The bus had begun to take a steep downhill turn, followed by yet another incline, when the driver finally shouted, "One hundred and twelfth Street!" But in the twilight and the snow, and the scant light along the Drive, there wasn't the slightest sign of 112th Street. I got off and watched my bus leave, wistfully, with the snow padding its lank shoulders as it shuffled off like an empty vessel headed toward destinations and sights unseen.

Facing me was a small, deserted, bushy knoll over which perched the statue of Samuel J. Tilden, the governor of New York famous for losing the 1876 presidency to Rutherford Hayes by one electoral vote.

I was, it occurred to me, in the middle of nowhere. Perhaps I shouldn't have come at all, I thought, feeling quite silly to be lugging a plastic bag in which two bottles of wine kept clinking despite the piece of cardboard the man at the liquor store had inserted between them. I decided to scale the hill and take a look. I heard the voices of children. A large Saint Bernard hovered nearby. And two boys came sliding down Tilden's incline on a makeshift sled. We were in a medieval village on the first night of winter.

Suddenly before me sprang the arrogant façade of a building I had spotted moments earlier on the bus, its lighted windows speckling like a constellation. Inside, I pictured quiet, contented households where children always started homework on time and where guests, ever reluctant to leave, enlivened dinners where spouses seldom spoke. Straight ahead, in the distance, loomed the Cathedral of St. John the Divine. It made me think of Leipzig and of Bach choirs and of the way the slightest accident sometimes opens up new worlds and new friendships we can no longer live without.

A doorman showed me to the elevator and, sticking his large uniformed arm behind the sliding door, pressed the button for me. I felt at once honored and inept. The old-style wooden elevator, with its miniature latticed dome and a beveled mirror framed in *faux* rosewood, spoke of Old World opulence gone tacky at the hands of rent-control landlords. Someone was already inside the elevator. She was wearing a dark blue raincoat, busily stamping snow off her boots. I caught myself wishing she was one of the guests. But she got off on another floor.

When the elevator door opened again, I instantly made out the muffled hubbub of a party. A tilting coatrack, filled to capacity, stood outside a door that had been purposely left ajar. I assumed this was the place. I wasn't expecting a large party. I should never have brought wine, I thought. I took off my coat and laid it on the hat rest, taking a moment before making my way in.

Inside my hosts' apartment someone had turned off the lights in the living room and everyone gave a startled "Ahh!" as we all stared at the lights on Riverside Drive. From the darkness within I caught sight of the glistening shoreline of New Jersey, and right below our building, in Riverside Park, solitary lampposts stood in glistening pools of silent light, each like a stranded ghost with its head ablaze. A lonely barge was sailing downstream—and as though shadowing

it on land, an M5 bus, with yellow lights on, drifted downtown as
well.

A while later that evening, the woman I'd seen on the elevator
suddenly reappeared, walking in with a large key ring which she
casually deposited in a brass bowl on the mantelpiece, clearly a
neighbor who'd been invited to dinner and had taken her time
arriving. It took us a minute to realize where we had already met.
She, like me, pretended not to remember. I took that as a good sign.

We sat next to each other on the sofa, and together went out to
smoke on the terrace, coming back to sit at the dining table, where
host and hostess, changing seating arrangements at the last minute,
had decided to put us together.

During coffee and dessert, fearing the spell might soon wear
off, I decided that, once I left that night, I would play the evening
in reverse, taking it back to the moment when I had purchased the
wine and inadvertently hopped on the M5 and watched one strange
block after the other unfold like a novel I had barely started and
hoped might never ever end. I remembered the Saint Bernard, and
the view of the cathedral, and the laughter of children sledding
down Tilden's mound that had made me think I had walked into
an enchanted town. All of these seemed part of a larger design, as
though each in its own small way had presaged our meeting and
would wait till late in the snow to hear of how things had gone
between us.

Later still, when it was time to leave, she showed me to the elevator; then she took me downstairs to the lobby and, perhaps
because it was such a beautiful night and the snow had begun to
subside and neither of us had finished talking, she borrowed the
doorman's umbrella and offered to accompany me to the corner of
Riverside and 112th Street, where she indicated the downtown

bus stop across the Drive. She asked once more whether I wouldn't prefer a taxi. I said no.

She walked me to the hillock and, nearing Tilden, shook my hand, the way the owner of a manor might escort her guest to a small unassuming gate and watch him walk away, with a last farewell chimed by the hidden bell once the gate closed.

Soon, like a carriage with a faithful coachman who'd been told to wait in a hidden stable nearby, an empty bus appeared. I sat behind the driver and watched him skip one stop after the other racing down the curves on Riverside. In no time we'd reached Seventy-second; the sound of her voice was still fresh in my mind.

I saw her again after that—always arriving on the M5, always hoping to land into that strange snowy night again, forever trying to coax her on certain evenings to take the bus with me while it was still winter, if only to share my imaginary Leipzig. But neither that winter nor the next did we walk out into the snow again.

That was many years ago. Ever since, I have taken the M5 out of curiosity, hoping for the day when I'd realize that perhaps I cared more for the bus ride and Leipzig and Samuel J. Tilden than I did for her, because there was more of me in these than there ever was in her.

Yet perhaps it wasn't even the bus ride I loved but the memory of those painful evenings when I'd find myself on the M5 and would let the bus pass by a stop that was no longer mine, sometimes only to change my mind and get off a few blocks up and amble back among the solitary lampposts, feeling very much like a stranded ghost with his head ablaze, scanning her windows and thinking back to my first night, and the last, and the night I thought I'd never be asked upstairs, and the night I feared my nights were numbered there, the night I felt unwanted but was nevertheless asked to stay, the night I suddenly looked outside and, if just to spite her, said I envied those strolling outside, the night I swore would be my last, the night I staked everything to have it be the first again, the night I longed to be alone, the night I feared I might soon be.

On those evenings, as on those moments in life when our hull is cracked and we're forced to molt everything we've got till we're as naked as a newborn and begin the slow, difficult work of reinventing a new skin with the very little we've got left each time, I felt so exposed that, like the isolated baby monkey in the experiment, I found that I could get attached to anything—a thought, a habit, a song; everything I touched or read or so much as leaned my head against became dearer to me than was the person in that apartment whose lights at night were more beguiling and intractable than a light from a vanished star.

I would let a few days pass. But I always came back. Perhaps I wanted to start all over again and thought that by dint of hopping on the M5 I might one day pass through the right portals of time and be asked to step back a year. Or perhaps I simply wanted to run into her on the bus, which never happened.

And yet, by taking the M5's route in the evening, I eventually got to know the buildings on Riverside one by one, projecting on each a different shade of lovesickness, forever enlisting the sympathy of asphalt and stone along this meandering stretch of Manhattan. I found myself giving each building a new tale, a new name, new residents, a different address even, not by altering its number, but by decrypting the unsuspected Bach cantata number or the

Mozart Köchel designation behind each one, because this was my way of warming up to them in a season when everything else felt so cold, because this was the closest I would ever come to piety or prayer, because this was my way of seeking order in chaos, my way of making a city that seemed so hostile and alien share something that was mine. Thus, the lanky number 80 on the corner of Riverside and Eightieth Street, known as the Riverside Tower Hotel, suddenly reminded me of Bach's 80th Cantata, *Ein feste Burg*, my favorite cantata (BWV 80); and number 140, on the corner of Eighty-sixth Street, the huge Art Deco building called the Normandy, so reminiscent of the French liner *Normandie*, which burned and was scuttled off a Manhattan pier, evokes Bach's *Wachet auf* (BWV 140), while across the street, at number 137, the stately, more conservative white forefront of the Clarendon, named after the seventeenth-century English memorialist who died in France, would draw me not only to *Lobe den Herren* (BWV 137), which I had never heard until then, but also to Mozart's Divertimento in B flat, otherwise known as K. 137. On Riverside and Eighty-fifth, however, Cantata 131—*Aus der Tiefe rufe ich, Herr*—lost to Beethoven's C Sharp major quartet, Opus 131, while I could never decide whether her building, 395 Riverside Drive, on the corner of 112th, belonged to Bach's *O Welt, sieh hier dein Leben* (BWV 395) or to Mozart's Capriccio for Piano (K. 395). Across the street, at 625 West 112th—the last building on West 112th Street, which I'd stare at from our windows every evening, because those who lived there seemed to live such serene lives while ours seemed to peter out by the day—something forever intrigued me: it was just one number shy of K. 626, the last piece of music Mozart would ever compose, his unfinished *Requiem Mass*. It occurs to me now that since we lived across the street, K. 626 would most probably have been us, had her corner building not had a Riverside Drive address instead. I keep promising to go and check one day. But I know I never will.

All I do instead is make up excuses simply to ride the M5: the scenic route, the road to memory, the yearning and dream-making as I let my mind drift when I ride up or down Riverside Drive, thinking of it as the ultimate urban promenade and wondering if there isn't something mildly shameful in being seen going out of my way to take public transportation. Sometimes, before going home, I get off the subway at Seventy-second and Broadway, and waiting in the milling crowd outside the last remaining subway house in Manhattan, I'll simply stand there, taking it all in, facing the vest-pocket park called Verdi Square, the Ansonia, and, farther right, the dull spill of lights off the eastern wall of the Apple Bank Building, and before me the two main arteries of the Upper West Side—Broadway and Amsterdam Avenue—knowing that when it's time to take the bus, I'll pretend, if only for an instant, that I have yet to make a quick stop, as I did on that day so many years ago, at a liquor store on Seventy-second Street. But the liquor store no longer exists, the way the Eclair, the West Side's famous Viennese pastry shop, no longer exists, the way the Embassy, our favorite movie theater, no longer exists either, swallowed as it was by a large co-op building called the Alexandria.

And as I continue to stand by the metal bar, which prevents pedestrians from spilling onto the busy intersection, I look northward and find that, strangely enough, I do not mind that all things must go, that the very spot where we ended up saying goodbye without even knowing we were saying goodbye that night was once a bar but is now a clothing store, having been a flower shop, then a grocery for a while. Indeed, staring at the fleet of buses which come up Broadway but must separate in four different directions on Seventy-second, I am suddenly filled not just with a sense of immense gratitude—gratitude to be alive in this city and at this moment, gratitude for the friends I've made, and for those I love—but also with a longing for all those unknown faces and unknown ways of getting to unknown spots in the city, all of them, now, the faces and places, known and unknown, forever beckoning in the evening light with what Stendhal, in his book *On Love*, once called a promise of bliss.

Three Tales

Pensione Eolo

❊

In 1984 I thought I'd be living in Europe. After more than fifteen years in the United States, the time had finally come for me to return to a continent I had long considered my home. I remember now the joy on first receiving the job offer by mail, a joy I held on to at first like a lover to a new love, secretly, repeating the news to no one, not even to myself, partly for fear of ruining the spell, and partly to renew that access of joy each time I managed to forget I had already opened that much-awaited letter, which began, not, as I forced myself to believe, with the familiar "We regret . . ." but with the insidious, baffling, treacherous "We are pleased to inform you . . ." These repeated bursts of joy made everything about that early-winter evening on the Upper West Side seem luminous, as though hazy premonitions of Europe had suddenly been released by the letter and were now infusing everything, from the late-autumnal cast of light on Broadway, to the sound of traffic, of people, down to the peculiar pre-dinner rush around Butler Library, where I liked to work before heading off to my favorite café on Amsterdam Avenue.

By virtue of pretending to suppress the joy, I had almost managed to unearth another emotion, one that doesn't have a name and which may be not even an emotion but the shadow of an emotion, and which hovered about like the other face of joy, its tactful underside, its surrogate, silent partner, something like an undefined languor which finally surfaced when I eventually managed to remind myself that, once in Europe, I'd be missing Christmas in New York that year.

I was longing for something I already had, all the while sensing that this manufactured nostalgia for New York was but another way of re-releasing a joy that had, by virtue of these antics and torsions, suddenly turned coy and reluctant on me.

For months I'd toyed with the thought of returning to Italy. I had pictured myself heading for an island which, by early fall, would already be cleared of tourists, though warm enough for a quick swim in the afternoon or an *al fresco* late dinner in what could still pass for a nightlife among the natives and hardened expats. A local café/trattoria, the return of the fishermen by sunset, the early-evening fog, the unavoidable emptying of the town square once it grows cold each year, those bleak hours spent correcting English- and French-language high-school homework by a weak light or, as I feared, under the powerful neon glare with which islanders sometimes hope to brighten their lives. Ours was to be a tiny, respectable hotel, Pensione Eolo, named after the god of the winds. From the windows you'd catch a glimpse of the tiny marina where the ferry stops twice each day. Pensione Eolo remains half-shut during the fall and winter months. On Sundays the locals would use the main dining room for family luncheons and wedding parties. Otherwise, all four of us would dine in a converted TV room with a large, communal table: a marine biologist, a music teacher from Hungary, and a young ex-nun from Trentino who teaches Latin and whom everyone calls Suor Angelica because she still intends to renew her vows. She and I would have adjacent rooms, but there'd be a partition in the balcony. Sometimes, while grading homework, a whiff of tobacco would waft through my open windows from hers. On Saturday evenings, she'd sit on her balcony and smoke, watching the crowd of young folks and families thin out as everyone headed for the only movie theater in this part of town. She says she doesn't like new movies. Sometimes I see her sitting by herself behind the glass window at Caffè Gianciotto, spooning a large tortoni. One day I'll have to ask her why she never gets lonely.

The mail here is unspeakably slow, and my lifeline to New York dries up every so many weeks. There is no local library. I must subscribe to *The New Yorker, The New York Review of Books,* and *New York* magazine. My mind turns back to the late sixties, when, as a student newly arrived in the United States, I continued to purchase French and Italian magazines so as not to let go of Europe, knowing all along, however, that I'd unavoidably lose touch and that despite my promises to hold on to the old, the new invariably had ways of demoting old things. I had already seen it happen once before, when, almost against my will, as an adolescent new to Italy, I had gradually begun to let go of Alexandria in favor of Rome.

Now, however, I began to fear that once in Europe I'd want to know exactly what was playing at the Met, at the Thalia, the Film Forum, the 92nd Street Y, or what new building had gone up on the Upper West Side, which restaurants had opened, which bookstores closed. I wanted to be there and witness whatever changes were bound to happen, and not just hear of them through friends, or have them spring on me when I'd eventually return. I wanted the city to go into deep hibernation, not breathe, not change, the way those who are about to die would like everyone alive to doze away with them in a collective slumber until the Day of Judgment, or the way spurned lovers want the world to stop loving and the places they remember with love in their hearts to remain intact, as they themselves promise to alter nothing in their lives, not the buses they used to ride or the clothes they used to wear, until the day their beloved is finally restored to them.

In this state of anticipated nostalgia, which is how those who fear homesickness try to immunize themselves against it—by experiencing it in small, persistent doses beforehand—I found myself missing *The New York Times* and, of all things, the one thing I never used to read regularly, the "Metropolitan Diary," where average New Yorkers report on the odd, jittery, unhinged character of life in the Big Apple. Would I really be able to withstand stumbling on this or that overheard conversation at such-and-such a familiar place and not ache to rush down a few blocks and see for myself?

Before I knew what I was doing, I had begun to jot down my own "Metropolitan Diary," little entries that tried to capture life and love on the Upper West Side. These were my *Zettelschriften*, snatches and snapshots of what was to be my own portable New York.

My notebooks were littered with these Manhattan marginalia: moments of being, spots of time, epiphanies: places in New York which, by virtue of my impending trip, were now retroprospectively blended into my little island off the western coast of Italy.

Thus, inspired by Joyce's brief "Giacomo Joyce," one day I wrote:

Suor Angelica: Thought of her again tonight as I stepped out of the 96th Street subway station. It was snowing when I came out. Walked an additional few blocks on my way home simply to think of her, toyed with my picture of Pensione Eolo: small, modest, out-of-season pensione, corner room mine, next to Suor Angelica's, overlooking the

marina. January: cardigan weather. Both of us teachers at
the nuns' school. We go by bike each day. Mother Superior
frowning at us—you are growing too familiar with each
other. She's right of course. Look the young ex-nun in the
eye, which gets her all perturbed, till Angelica finally drops
me a note on my way to class one day, furtive must-see-you-
immediately, *in confidenza*, she says. She doesn't mind I'm
late when I knock. What courage, though, when she says she
may still wish to renew her vows. Forgot people could shake
like that. How different, how infinitely more passionate than
P., who's busy leafing through stacks of balance sheets in the
bedroom, the TV turned on loud, knowing it disturbs me,
waiting for me to apologize about something or other, which
I still won't do, as I sit and invent this woman in Italy whose
one flustered glance, as she debates the matter of her vows,
is worth a hundred nights in Manhattan.

What I was doing was throwing myself *out there*, into the
future, only to turn around and seize the here and now. Perhaps
what I wanted all along was New York. Or perhaps what I wanted
was to think that I liked New York, or that I could only think so provided I spun the world enough times not to have to know whether I
belonged anywhere.

Expatriation, like love, is not only a condition that devastates and
reconfigures the self; it is, like love, a trope, a figure with which we
try to explain, to narrate profound psychological disruptions in
terms of very measurable entities: a person, a place, an event, a
moment, etc.

Nostalgia is one such metaphor.

By missing Manhattan, I learn to long for it, to love it, though I am now conscious that I'm losing Manhattan because I'm about to revisit a place I've always suspected I loved more than Manhattan but will not really allow myself to think I'll be able to revisit unless it, too, like Manhattan, becomes a site of nostalgia, something I can lose, might lose, have lost. Place, in this very peculiar context, means something only if it is tied to its own displacement. I posit one point, but then I posit a second, which sends me back to the first, which then sends me back again to the second, and so on. Nothing is stable; every signal emitted turns on me and comes back with the same questioning glance with which it was emitted. Everything becomes a mirror image of itself and of something else. I am, insofar as I can speak of an I, a tiny thinking image caught in a hall of mirrors, thinking, among other things, about halls of mirrors. I am, for all I know, a hall of mirrors.

The problem, clearly enough, is not with place but with me, insofar as place and identity are meshed here in such a way that I may say that I am always, always caught between two points, one of which is always a metaphor of the other. But that's not quite correct. I am not caught between two points. I *am* two points caught in the same spot. Correction: I am two points caught in different spots.

This may explain why I am always fond of using the image, the *figure*, of two foci in an ellipse, or of the two banks of a river, or of the many strands in a cat's cradle that always manage to reproduce generations of patterns with baffling regularity. The figure in all this is always the same: me tussling between two shadow centers.

I have tried to give a flavor of this figure in many ways *here*: by showing that once I'm in Italy, I'd really be in New York; that when I'm in New York, I'm already in Italy. In fact, this figure was already present when I described how my superstitious attempts to come to terms with the job offer abroad had almost made me reluctant to accept it, and how, by virtue of countenancing this rejection, I was in fact propitiating my acceptance, even though these propitiatory motions had a way of diluting my desire to leave New York by reintroducing the desire to return, and, in so doing, diluting the joy of leaving till it became a loathing to leave.

The French moralists would have called these antics not just a *renversement continuel* of one thing for another but, more precisely, a traffic, a commerce, an economy.

Commerce and economy give a transactional character to the psyche; traffic, on the other hand, is much more accurate, because it captures the confused, back-and-forth, up-and-around, congested nature of ambivalence, of love, and of nostalgia. Traffic captures the bizarre nature of the psyche, where the dominant motion is one not so much of ambivalence as of perpetual oscillation. The true *site* of nostalgia is therefore not a land, or two lands, but the loop and interminable traffic between these two lands. It is the traffic between places, and not the places themselves, that eventually becomes the home, the spiritual home, the capital. Displacement, as an abstract concept, becomes the tangible home. Let me in fact borrow an adjective from Heraclitus to give this traffic of multiple turns and returns a name by calling it *palintropic*. To quote Diels's Fragment 51: "They do not comprehend how a thing agrees at variance with itself; it is an attunement turning back on itself, like that of the bow and the lyre."

"Palintropic" means that which "turns again—which keeps turning," which loops back or "turns back on itself" or is "backstretched"—a going back to oneself, a flipping back to oneself, a sort of systemic *renversement* reminiscent of the back-sprung

reflex Homeric bow, which was strung in such a way as to counter-
act the normal curvature of the bow, reversing the curve to gain
more power.

This, if I might suggest, is the seat of nostalgia, perhaps not its
origin but certainly its end point. This is my home, my emotional,
aesthetic, and intellectual home.

My home is a counterhome, and my instincts are counter-
instincts. Yet this is my home, my emotional, aesthetic, and intellectual home. Exile, nostalgia, a broken heart, and other profound
reversals mean nothing unless they induce a corresponding set of
intellectual, psychological, and aesthetic reversals as well. I project
these reversals on everything, because it is in finding reversals that
I am able to find myself. I consolidate my palintropic relationship
with the world by redefining the world as a palintropic construct. I
cannot "access" the world and cannot find my bearings in it, I cannot behave in the world nor can I narrate the world unless I've
unearthed its palintropic moment. A palintropic reading of the
world assumes that one is not quite like others and that to understand others, to be with others, to love others and be loved by
them, one must think *other* thoughts than those that come naturally to one. To be with others I must be the opposite of who I am;
to understand others, I must read the opposite of what I see, say
the opposite of what I mean, think the opposite of what I feel, ask
for what I do not want. I might as well be someone else.

And I find this moment, this figure everywhere. I find it, for
example, in the life of Emperor Julian the Apostate, who converted
from paganism to Christianity, then back to paganism; or in the life
of another apostate, Uriel da Costa, Spinoza's near-contemporary,
born into a *converso* family in Portugal, who later converted to
Judaism in Amsterdam, then back to Catholicism, and back to
Judaism again, ultimately committing suicide; in the life of the seer

Tiresias, who was born a man, became a woman, and became a man again; I find it in my ancestors, who had left Spain to go to Italy, from Italy to Turkey, then back to Italy, some ultimately going to Israel, only to leave the Promised Land to seek out Italy once more. They were at first Jewish, then *conversos*, then Jews again, some turning to the Christian faith, as my family did, for political reasons, only to turn back to a form of diluted Judaism that longed for a lost Christian past. I find it in the history of my own city, Alexandria, which after being an international commercial center in antiquity was conquered by the Arabs, to become an international city fifteen hundred years later under Western rule, only to return to the Arabs. The history of the Middle East from Troy to Jerusalem is, needless to say, filled with similar instances. I am thrilled when I see street performers who stand still in the middle of sidewalk traffic, imitating a stationary human statue, which itself imitates the human body.

I find it in Stendhal, whose characters, whose voice, and whose prose earn the right to grow sentimental provided they have repressed their initial effusion with gestures of irony. Intuition is always counterintuitive.

I find it in the story I invented about Ulysses, who, suspecting that once he's returned to Ithaca he may miss his days as an immortal in Calypso's arms, determines never to leave Calypso and chooses immortality instead. Ulysses, who realizes in fact that nostalgia is not some sort of restless energy that propels him homeward, but that nostalgia is his home, the way that, in exile, only paradox makes sense. He finds his home in the purely intellectual realization that he has no home. The site of nostalgia is nostalgia itself. The site of nostalgia is writing and speculating and thinking about nostalgia.

At the end of *Du côté de chez Swann* and at the beginning of *A l'ombre des jeunes filles en fleurs*, the adolescent Marcel meets Gilberte Swann in a garden on the Champs-Elysées and is totally taken with her. It should be remembered that this comes just after the Prousts have decided to vacation in Italy one Easter but have since had to change plans: the thrill of going to Italy has so excited the frail Marcel that a family physician forbids the boy to travel to Italy at all. Hence the Champs-Elysées garden, and hence also the eventual displacement of Marcel's dreams of Venice and Florence by the more ordinary trips each year to Combray.

Combray was always an *alibi*, an elsewhere, a second-best behind which hovered Marcel's incessant yet ever-thwarted dreams of Italy. That Marcel should have met the love of his life in Combray, and not Venice, and that he should have had his first parasexual encounter on the Champs-Elysées and not in Italy, and that his dreams and eventual visit to Venice should have been punctuated with powerful and uncanny reminders of Combray, and finally that he should realize at the end of *Albertine disparue* that what life had to offer him was exactly what he had always wanted if only he had known how to ask for it and seize it when it was offered to him in the least likely of places, Combray, all these ironies and counterintuitive revelations underwrite the fundamentally palintropic texture of Proust's novel. Life's painful ironies and coincidences in Proust have ways of becoming "beautiful" and meaningful once they are transferred onto paper, Proust's true home. *The site of nostalgia is nostalgia itself.* Paper displaces place, the way writing displaces living.

In *A l'ombre des jeunes filles en fleurs*, Marcel is seen passing by the seemingly inaccessible Swann residence and imagines what it must feel like to be an habitué there. As far as he can tell, everything about the forbidding Swann household seems to bar him access. But one day Marcel is finally invited. He is invited several times. So that now he can look out the window and, as though to complete the cycle, try to remember what it must have felt like to have been an outsider once. This move out in the opposite direction not only holds the illusory promise of making him whole but is his way of savoring and resavoring his success. What he finds, however, is that one of the rewards of that success is no longer to be able to remember having longed for it. By another quirk of irony, however, failure to feel whole for the tortured Proustian sensibility is, in fact, a mark of being whole. The pain of realizing that one is fundamentally at odds with the world is ultimately tempered, if not reversed, by the mental agility with which this piece of information is arrived at and ultimately logged down.

Behind all this, of course, hovers the ultimate reversal in the vague inklings that, with Gilberte's growing indifference, Marcel will soon be on the outside looking in again.

Proustian love always follows an air-with-three-voices pattern. From extremes of loneliness to intimacy and back to loneliness. From indifference to intense jealousy, underscored, as always, by the predictable return of indifference. It's not that indifference, like loneliness, suddenly reappears; it's that it has never really gone away. Nor is it that it competes with its opposite, vying with desire for center stage. Irony—Proustian, Stendhalian, Svevian, Ovidian, Austenian—is not characterized so much by the subversion of one voice by another as by an ongoing perpetual traffic between them. It is frequently called a dialectic. It is not. A dialectic is progressive, digressive. Palintropic traffic is static. It's not that you cannot come back home; it's that you've never really left anything to have to come back to.

The critic Edwin Muir, who was not insensitive to this figure, picked it up in a scene in Laurence Sterne's *Sentimental Journey* and, quite appropriately, called it Proustian. In that scene, a man holds a woman's hand and, anticipating her reaction to his "slight compression of her palm," reads in her imagined reaction a certain reluctance, thereby opting not to press her hand at all.

You anticipate the reaction to your own gesture and react to the other's reaction before initiating your own. The palintropic traffic, needless to say, is potentially infinite. There are authors who devote their whole attention to that traffic, and hardly any to plot. There are authors who write that way: by the time they're about to write something, they've already thought of its correction. The first thing they write, the original version, is the correction. They are, to use Nietzsche's words, always "trying to cover up their feet." As a result, the text is always nostalgic for those stillborn versions of itself that were crossed out before being written down. In fact, palintropic movement has no origin. You cannot leave, but you already long for the place from which you intend to leave. Nostalgia is rooted in the text itself. That Proust, for example, should allude to his text as a translation is no accident; *A la recherche* is a transposition of an entire lifetime onto paper. The text is nostalgic for the life it is to be a transcription of. But it is just as much a transcription of that life's own desire to work itself into a book. To put it in very simple terms: the desire to write *A la recherche* is what the narrator's life was all about. The real nostalgia, therefore, is not for Combray, or for an evasive Venice behind Combray, or for a lost childhood, but for the book that was to record the passage from Combray to Venice and from Venice to Combray all over again. The real nostalgia is not for a place but for the *record* of that nostalgia. The real nostalgia has no point of origin; it is dispersed in the palintropic traffic between several points.

Ultimately, the real site of nostalgia is not the place that was lost or the place that was never quite had in the first place; it is the text that must record that loss. In fact, the act of recording the loss is the ultimate homecoming, inasmuch as the act of recording one's inability to find one's home on going back to it becomes a homecoming as well. Reading about this paradox is a homecoming. Musing and trying to sort out this paradox is a homecoming. In Proust, even showing how everything is always in the wrong place whenever we go looking for it in the right place is ultimately a way of finding the right thing for the wrong reasons in the right place at the wrong time—which, all told, is very much a homecoming as well.

Let me take this a step further: the true site of nostalgia is not the original place (since there really isn't one), nor is it just the text that will eventually record the absence of such an origin, or ponder the implied paradox of this. Nor is it the come-and-go traffic between one place and another, or between the text and its multiple versions. The true site of nostalgia is, of course, all of the above—coupled, however, with the realization that to be successful every literary return and every literary reminiscence, like every Proustian insight, must be incomplete and always eager to consider its own failure as such.

I never went to Italy that year. Pensione Eolo remained a whirlpool of fictions and fantasies and of the memory of an imagined winter spent with a defrocked nun, a marine biologist, and a Hungarian musicologist. I remember as though it were yesterday the day I pictured myself running to the ferryboat one evening to get my mail, only to find that none had arrived that day. The woman in New York whose letters I would have craved to read in Italy was in the next room sulking, while I, in her living room, would look outside over to

Riverside Park like a prisoner imagining his imminent liberation, envying those lucky enough to be alone in the park that weekday evening. I hadn't even told her I had applied for a job abroad. I simply wanted to get away, and kept looking for the slightest pretext to tell her that we couldn't live together, that she should look for someone else, that I couldn't wait to be back where I thought I'd be among my own.

What I didn't know was that the woman sulking in the other room was not only already in love with another man but had herself made plans for an extended summer vacation with him in, of all places, Italy.

How better to prevent her from leaving than by not leaving myself? I decided to stay. She, however, left.

That winter, when it was all over, I would walk or ride a bus past her building. Sometimes I'd think how lucky I'd been to have spent a year with her there and how gladly I would give everything I now had to be back with the same woman, staring out those windows whenever she went sulking into the other room, imagining and envying those strolling outside, never once suspecting that one day soon I might be a stroller, too, looking in, envying the man I'd been there once, knowing all along, though, that if I had to do it over again, I'd still end up where I was, yearning for those days when I was living with a woman I had never loved and would never love but in whose home I had managed to fall in love with an ex-would-be-nun whose presence was indissolubly fused to an apartment on the Upper West Side that became dearer to me and made me love New York because from these rooms I had looked out of windows facing the Hudson and invented a woman who, like me, was neither here nor there.

Arbitrage

⁂

One afternoon in 1973, during the Indian summer days of my first semester of graduate school, I went to visit a girl who had invited me to her studio after a seminar. She had invited me for tea, but I assumed that it was really for something else, only to find, when we sat down on her sofa, that I'd actually been invited to help her write an overdue paper on Wordsworth's "Tintern Abbey." Seeing that I showed signs of reluctance, her features became flustered, and, without warning, she burst out sobbing. I felt sorry for her and held her in my arms until the crying subsided. When I finally agreed to help, she got up swiftly, disappeared into the kitchen, took out an old-fashioned kettle, and put some water on to boil. Then she led me to a gnarled wooden table that stood against a wall, pulled out two chairs, and, after lighting a cigarette, which made me think that we would be working on this together for quite some time, suddenly stubbed it out, remembering that she had plans to see someone else that evening. Would I mind terribly helping with the paper while she was gone? Sullenly I said I didn't mind. An uncomfortable moment of silence passed between us. I was welcome to wait for her if I wanted, she offered as she hastily slipped on her coat. A few seconds later the large glass panel on the front door downstairs gave a loud, resounding clank.

Still dazed by the speed with which one thing had led to another, I thought about how she had folded a baby-blue paper napkin and set it ever so gently under my teaspoon, saying, with goading irony, before rushing to the door, *For the sugar, for the tea, for the writer*, as if to suggest with this tiny gesture of solicitude that she wasn't the inconsiderate sort. I lit a cigarette and let my eyes roam around the tiny studio she had frequently mentioned but which corresponded to nothing I had expected. From her table, I looked out onto the corner of Mount Auburn and Linden Streets, as the approaching late-summer evening slowly settled on the adjoining rooftops. A crowd of students was straggling back from the libraries, some headed for early dinners. The studio, small, cluttered, and overheated despite the open windows, seemed strangely trusting, candid, and, like a child who's been told to entertain a stranger while Mother's getting dressed upstairs, it dutifully reminded me to help myself to anything I pleased: make more tea, look for treats—there were bound to be *things*, she'd said, indicating the refrigerator and a tiny kitchen cabinet, which she had flung open both to encourage me to do likewise when she was gone and to indicate, with feigned absentmindedness, that its contents were as unfamiliar to her as they'd be to anyone who happened to drop by. It took me a while to realize that her exaggerated ignorance of her kitchen was simply her way of showing that she was casual about everything else in her life.

Everything she owned was on show: her notebooks, her sweaters, Bach's *Saint Matthew Passion* clumsily splayed on the floor, a striped ironing board standing next to her bed, a Greek icon, and a domed photo enlarger relegated to the periphery of the room like a demoted hanger-on. Among this scatter of objects was the teapot, over which she had placed a quilted tea cozy. In the cloying comfort of this hot room, the presence of that unusual piece of quilting suddenly thrust me back a decade earlier to the languid *fin d'été* world of my childhood in Alexandria, where my aging after-school tutors, who began wearing wool early in the fall each year, had sipped tea at my desk. The tiny studio now felt so familiar, so welcoming in its Old World warmth, that I almost forgot it belonged to a flamboyant jet-setter with whom every man in our class claimed to have had the same adventure.

And so, as I poured the tea the way my tutors had done, I began to feel not happy but exceptionally sheltered and snug in this studio. I wanted to be there for a long time and neglected even to take myself to task for not having seized the moment when I'd held her in my arms, knowing that she'd have kissed me passionately if only I'd been bolder. I liked this room. I knew this room. Perhaps a tiny part of me was already lodged here and wished to come back again and again in the days to come, in search of that moment just after sunset when, switching on the first light and letting the windows turn to mirrors against the darkening sky, I'd watch Cambridge disappear and Alexandria suddenly rise upon the windowpanes.

The paper on "Tintern Abbey" was not difficult to write. I had written my own paper a week before and had already said all I could think of saying about the poem, so this was to be done more in the spirit of an evening ramble, something I didn't really have to write and wouldn't be graded on. Part of me didn't much care, especially since I was feeling a tad spiteful. And yet there *was* a moment of inspiration, though I hadn't quite registered it yet—something in Wordsworth and me and this girl and this studio and the act of recognizing all too readily now, years after leaving Egypt, years after reading Proust and Leopardi, the unmistakable signals that a memory was about to blossom there.

While I was writing, I'd get up every once in a while, to drink some water, go to the bathroom, or snoop around the studio. I remember how scant the light was and how startling it seemed to me, even at the time, that this strange, dark, quiet room and this girl and the student I was then were in many more ways than I realized tied together by a poem by Wordsworth entitled "Lines Composed a Few Miles Above Tintern Abbey, on Revisiting the Banks of the Wye During a Tour."

On the eve of Bastille Day, July 13, 1798, the twenty-eight-year-old Wordsworth went with his sister to Tintern Abbey, on the Wye River, a place that he had already visited five years before. That same evening, Wordsworth sat down to write a poem celebrating his return:

> Five years have passed; five summers, with the length
> Of five long winters! and again I hear
> These waters, rolling from their mountain-springs
> With a soft inland murmur.—Once again
> Do I behold these steep and lofty cliffs,
> That on a wild secluded scene impress
> Thoughts of more deep seclusion . . .

The poem he writes, however, celebrates not only the present moment but also his previous visit in 1793, as well as the future memory of both visits.

While here I stand, not only with the sense
Of present pleasure, but with pleasing thoughts
That in this moment there is life and food
For future years . . .

Wordsworth fears losing that future memory, and at the end of the
poem he tells his sister that, if he dies, she should remember their
visit *for him.*

> Nor, perchance—
> If I should be where I no more can hear
> Thy voice, nor catch from thy wild eyes these gleams
> Of past existence—wilt thou then forget
> That on the banks of this delightful stream
> We stood together; and that I, so long
> A worshipper of Nature, hither came
> Unwearied in that service . . .

Wordsworth at Tintern Abbey, it occurred to me, was doing
more or less what I was doing in this girl's room: firming up the
present by experiencing it as a memory, by experiencing it from the
future as a moment in the past. What Wordsworth remembers at
Tintern Abbey is not the past but himself in the past imagining the
future; and what he looks forward to is not even the future but himself, in the future, retrieving the bone he buried in the past. He
purchases at the Exchange of Time what he sells at the Exchange of
Place, knowing that, at the end of the transaction, he'll borrow
from Place to purchase from Time to sell back to Place all over
again.

This, in the world of finance, is called "arbitrage": the purchase of securities in one market for resale in another. As soon as a profit is made, the cycle starts again, with subsequent purchases sometimes paid for with unrealized credit drawn from previous sales. In such transactions, one never really sells a commodity, much less takes delivery of anything. One merely speculates, for seldom does any of it have anything to do with the real world. Arbitrageurs have seats on not one but two exchanges, the way the very wealthy have homes not in one but in two time zones, or exiles two homes in the wrong places. One always longs for the other home, but home, as one learns soon enough, is a place where one imagines or remembers *other* homes.

Wordsworth was quite given to such mnemonic arbitrage. He builds on air, the way futures traders speculate on margin; he grounds the present on the past, and the future on the past recaptured. His system is elliptical: to use focus A you need to establish focus B, but to establish B you need A. The very *act* of anticipating an epiphany becomes the epiphany itself.

In some cases, Wordsworth even layered the anticipation of that epiphany with the recollection of similar anticipations, and hence epiphanies, in the past. It has been speculated that Wordsworth may even have visited Tintern Abbey in 1791. This would mean that in 1793, five years before he returned to Tintern Abbey with his sister, Wordsworth was already remembering an earlier visit. In 1793 he had in fact started a poem about Salisbury Plain, a place he had visited two years before, which suggests that, in 1798, when he finally composed "Tintern Abbey," he was repeating an earlier mnemonic experience. His last visit to Tintern Abbey, incidentally, was to take place in 1841. In that year Wordsworth did not write a poem. What we have instead are these words from a letter he sent to his friend Robinson:

Thence we came along the Wye the banks of which noble river I was truly glad to revisit—to Tintern Abbey where last Tuesday we had the great pleasure of meeting Miss Fenwick and Dora.

From the man who wrote what is arguably the most moving poem in English Romantic literature, and probably the most eloquent poem on memory ever written, this sounds almost intentionally flat. Perhaps it was not intentional at all. Perhaps this is simply how an aging and bewildered Wordsworth responded to a situation that had become far too gnarled for his poetic imagination. Wordsworth had already written his elegy on returning to Tintern Abbey. To write about Tintern Abbey again in 1841 he would have had to write a poem invoking not only his present visit but also his 1793 and 1798 visits (and possibly his 1791 visit).

I finished my essay on Wordsworth and, after tearing off the striped yellow sheets of paper and stapling them neatly on the girl's table, I proceeded to the next page of the notebook. Without giving the matter any thought, I began to write a story about going back to a place that was my own Tintern Abbey. Alexandria.

In the story, a young man returns to Alexandria. This, however, is by no means a momentous return journey. He is back in Alexandria because the ship on which he was sailing to Greece has made an unscheduled stop for repairs. While minor work is being done to the vessel, he decides to take advantage of the fortuitous layover and proceeds to stroll about a city he knew a decade ago. He is wearing dark flannel trousers and a rumpled white shirt. For lack of anywhere else to go, he finds himself drawn to the city's Jewish cemetery, where he decides to pay a visit to his grandfather's grave. The road is very dusty, as all unpaved Mediterranean roads are. Standing outside the Jewish cemetery, he taps at the gate, hears no answer, and taps again harder. Finally, the warden grumbles behind the door and opens it. The place looks exactly as he remembered it: a row of trees, a gravel path, a pebbled alleyway between the graves, and serene morning silence within. He looks around at the old tombstones and then—perhaps to make conversation—asks the aging caretaker how he makes ends meet, given that there are no visitors or Jewish "clients" left in Alexandria. The warden points to an old Coca-Cola icebox. Students heading to and from the university sometimes come in for a Coke. This is Alexandria's cemetery row, and people stop by. As they talk, the young man hears the cackle of a brood of chickens picking their way between the graves. Like many Bedouins in Egypt, the warden also earns a living by selling fresh eggs.

The young man and the warden proceed to look for the grandfather's grave. Neither of them has any idea where to find it. On impulse, the man thinks back to the last time he went to the cemetery—ten years before, with his father—and, as if by a miracle, he suddenly finds himself threading between the odd-shaped tombstones and locating the one he is looking for. It occurs to him as he stares at the inscription on the marble that, unless he makes an effort to remember where it is, he'll never be able to find this grave again, should he return in years to come. The notion amuses him, because he doubts he'll ever come back again.

The warden, who had gone back into his hut, returns with a bucket of water for him to clean the marble slab. He pours the water slowly, going at the task with unexpected zeal, perhaps in order to avoid asking himself why he's come here at all or what he expected to find. He gives the warden's son some change and asks him to get a Coca-Cola. The boy rushes behind the hut and comes back, holding a bottle awkwardly in both hands, as though he were carrying a struggling hen by the neck. Once the young man is in possession of the bottle, he does something he remembers his father telling him he should never do: he places it on the gleaming flat marble, heaves himself up, and sits on the warm slab. It is a beautiful sunny day. He is sweating. He knows it will only get hotter. He lights a cigarette. His feet are dangling from his perch. He could just as easily be sitting on the edge of a swimming pool.

And as the young man sits on the slab under the scant shade offered by one of the adjoining palm trees, his thoughts turn to the beach, to the beaches of Egypt especially, and to the way he has remembered them over the last ten years, first from Italy and then from New York. He realizes suddenly, in a sort of delayed double take, that if he looks over the cemetery wall he will see his favorite body of water in the world, lying scarcely two minutes away.

The last time he stood by this marble slab, he remembers, he was thinking about Italy, a country he feared and had never seen. His father had already purchased their tickets on an Italian liner, and an uncle had promised to meet them in Naples. Now, thinking about Egypt's beaches makes him long for the fountains of Rome, especially on those dry, scorching Italian summer days when a fountain is all the beach an impoverished exile can get.

During our three years in Italy immediately following our expulsion from Egypt, my parents had so little money that my mother had to alter my father's old clothes for me to wear. The task kept her busy for weeks. He owned several pairs of flannel trousers, and these were the easiest to spare. Thus, I found myself, like the young man of my story, wearing thick gray wool trousers into late spring each year, and I came to dread their unbearable prickly nap, especially when it grew hot, learning to read in my discomfort the first, unmistakable hints of summer. One day, years later, wearing wool trousers in New York, I felt a flush of almost sexual pleasure course along my thighs: it was not that I liked the heat but that it suddenly brought me back to those days in Rome when the pall of wool would send me in search of a fountain, where I could entertain the illusion that I was one step closer to the beach and—if the illusion lasted—to our summer house in Egypt, to my friends and my relatives, and to an entire world I longed to recover: the city I had known as a child, the smells, the heat, the cast of light, the taste of ripe fruit on summer mornings, the sound of a car rolling on gravel with its engine turned off, even the sounds of the flies and of itinerants, or of the city on crowded squares after Sunday Mass. All I needed during those years in Italy was a mild sense of thirst, wool pants, and a quiet, watery spot that muffled the sound of the city and gave the impression that if the day were clearer, a luminous Alexandria, with its beaches, sunlight, odors, and people, would surface suddenly, like the wide expanse of sea facing Xenophon's soldiers on their desperate journey back through Asia Minor. I learned to love Rome the roundabout way, by investing in it the nostalgia I felt for Alexandria, and the wool, the heat, and the sweat were as welcome a price to pay as is the foul odor of horse dung around Claremont Stable on West Eighty-ninth Street to a new city dweller who spent his childhood on a farm.

This is mnemonic arbitrage. Not only did I discover in a girl's studio in Cambridge a sensation I had experienced in Rome which evoked Alexandria but, in writing about Egypt in New York City years after that, I found myself remembering impressions that took me back not to Alexandria but to Rome, and ultimately to Cambridge.

Reverse arbitrage is no less unwieldy: when I eventually returned to Egypt in 1995, I caught myself looking at my beloved Mediterranean through tiny side streets and felt a sudden yearning for West End Avenue, looking toward the Hudson River through 106th Street—which had become my dearest spot on earth precisely because it reminded me of Alexandria. I was, in Alexandria, homesick for a place from which I had learned to re-create Alexandria, the way the rabbis, in exile, were forced to reinvent their homeland on paper, only to find, perhaps, that they worshipped the paper more than the homeland or the way that prisoners who express their love for the free world by painting its portrait on their cell wall come to worship the walls and not the world.

In my story at the cemetery, when the sun grows too oppressive the young man gets down from his perch and heads toward the warden's hut. Guessing that the warden hasn't been tipped in recent years, he puts his hand in his pocket and gives the man a twenty-dollar bill—probably more than a month's salary for the warden, who accepts it reluctantly. He wishes to offer the young man another Coke in return. The young man is reminded of the unfair exchange of armor between Glaucus and Diomedes and accepts the Coke.

But then the warden goes back into the hut and comes out with a tiny object, wrapped in what looks like an old kerchief. It's an antique silver cigarette lighter, with an inscription. Probably left behind by a Jewish mourner years before. Perhaps that mourner had come back in the same way, dawdled about for a while, smoked a cigarette, and then left, forgetting the lighter. To the young man's surprise, the inscription on the lighter bears all three of his initials. He knows that the lighter isn't his. He has never owned such a lighter. Had the other gentleman left it for him? The young man had come to the cemetery in search of something; and this is all he found.

Campy, to be sure, but this is the mystery, or the epiphany, my imagination concocted on that Indian-summer night in Cambridge. It would take me years to understand the meaning of the gift I had invented. The lighter could only have belonged to the young man—who was, of course, me. He/I *had* returned to the cemetery before though we hadn't realized it. We had been taking turns going back there every day for years, each time leaving our lighter in the Bedouin's care to remind each other that part of us would be forever left behind in Egypt, that part of us had never and would never take the ship but was irretrievably elsewhere.

I never really finished the story. On another Indian-summer afternoon, four years later, I picked it up again, and looking at its faded canary sheets, I could recollect exactly where I'd been sitting in that studio on Linden Street. I remembered the cast of light, the heat, and my unsettling sense that I'd been had that day. I labored over the story for two months, before finally abandoning it. It had become too elaborate, clothed in too many memories as in the history of its own revisions.

I returned to it once more under different circumstances on yet another warm Indian-summer day in a different city. I was sitting on a terrace and had used writing about my return to a sunny day in Egypt as a way of re-creating an imaginary summer day in childhood. It was when I turned my chair away from the sun that I suddenly recalled that glare in Egypt is so powerful that you are forced to squint or stare down and avoid looking at anything, which is why you can't stare at the sea and why the act of not staring at an imaginary sea anywhere else in the world was the surest sign that there was in fact so vast a body of water nearby.

In the story as I rewrote it that day, the young man is reminded of the beaches of his childhood, not because his legs are dangling as they would at a swimming pool, but because the glare from the marble tombstone leaves him momentarily blinded, as the glare from the sea once had.

I think that my love for the splendid vistas of the sea began not, as I have always liked to think, on the beaches of Alexandria, not in Egypt at all, but on that terrace, the way I learned to love the sun, not as a native, but as a tourist, or to love the summer, not in June, but in October. I wanted to take this love, which had blossomed in Rome, in New York, and in Cambridge, and graft it back onto the city I had known as a child. I wanted to repatriate my memories, ship everything back home, including the history of my apprenticeship that Indian-summer evening, when, in taking the long and roundabout passageways of memory to the girl's studio in Cambridge, I brought almost everything I had known and become into one room.

I wrote around this story for two decades. Over the years, it was the one story I thought about whenever I thought of writing; it hovered over me like an unclaimed ghost begging for an honorable burial. More insidiously, that unfinished story gradually changed the meaning of writing for me. My inability to rewrite the story mirrored my inability to return to Egypt, and I began to feel that the acts of writing and returning were bound in such intricate ways that without returning I would never be able to write anything at all, but that returning would close the book on Egypt before I'd done so on paper itself.

Egypt itself had become a metaphor, the way losing Egypt was a metaphor, the way reclaiming Egypt, or even trying to forget Egypt, was no less of a metaphor than writing about it. I had invented another Egypt, a mirror Egypt, an Egypt meant to be speculated about, an Egypt that stood beyond time, because although it gave every indication of having been lost, there was scant evidence that it had ever existed, an Egypt I kept frozen, tucked, secret, cosseted, an Egypt "on margin," an Egypt "on spec," an Egypt I "castled" with every other place I might have called home, an Egypt from the past that kept intruding on the present to remind me among so many other things that if I loved summoning the past more than the past I summoned up, and if it was not really Egypt I loved but remembering Egypt, this was also because my trouble was no longer with Egypt but with life itself. Not knowing how to let go of things was nothing more than the mirror image of not knowing how to take them when they were offered, for my deepest fear of all, which came to me obliquely that evening in Cambridge as I thought of Wordsworth and of this girl whose life seemed so rooted in the present, was of living directly under the noonday sun, without the shadows of past or future.

Many years later, walking with my brother on the Upper West Side one Sunday afternoon, I tried to explain to him how standing on that spot on West End Avenue looking toward the Hudson reminded me so much of our childhood and how I felt closer to him there than I had in a long time, but I sensed that he had no patience for this and fell silent.

I wanted to tell my brother that this spot on West End Avenue would always be special to me, that in years to come I'd make a point of returning here, that if I failed to come back again he should remember it for me. I wanted to tell him that I had learned all this, not in Egypt, not in Italy, not in Cambridge, not in New York, but in Wordsworth, and that if I ever wrote my book about Egypt I already knew I would have to end it with Wordsworth, with my brother and me standing in Alexandria, looking out to sea, already thinking of that evening when, years hence, whether in Europe or in America, we'd think back on our last night in Alexandria and, if we could, catch our own gaze going out the other way.

But my brother had no use for Egypt as metaphor. That evening I looked at "Tintern Abbey" in an old Scott Foresman anthology of British literature I had purchased on my last day of school before leaving Egypt. I had used the same volume in my senior year in Rome, as well as in a freshman course in college, but for me the poem is forever locked in that one evening in Cambridge, where, after writing a paper for a girl and emptying my third cup of Earl Grey from an old teapot she had placed on the table for me, I looked out the window over that strange darkened side street, from which dun-colored tones of dusk had crept over everything in the room, and rather than put my pen away, perhaps because I wanted an excuse to stay a little longer, or perhaps because I had just seen a connection that came to me in the form of a parable, I began scribbling a tale which, over the years, evolved into a book not just about memories of Egypt but about all the times I had remembered Egypt once I had left Egypt. I wrote this story both to remember Egypt and to put Egypt behind me, but also to revisit all those times when I'd looked for Egypt in Italy or in Cambridge or in New York, in Wordsworth or in Dante or in Homer or in Proust, and, most recently, in Egypt itself.

In October 1995, after the publication of *Out of Egypt*, I finally did go back to Alexandria and decided to visit the Jewish cemetery, not just for my grandfather's and my father's sakes but as a way of returning to the scene I had imagined in Cambridge almost twenty years earlier. Uncannily enough, everything I had invented in the short story was borne out by experience: the warden, my inability to locate the grave, the washing of the tombstone, the silence around me interrupted by the distant clank of tram wheels, the warden's child, the dog, and the dusty, dusty road. When I did eventually find the tombstone, it was only because I remembered how I'd discovered it in the story. I had returned to fiction—or had, at least, stepped into a realm where memory and imagination traded places with the dizzying agility of an entrechat.

There were a few differences: there was no slab on which to sit and enjoy the warm autumnal light that afternoon. Nor was there anything to drink. I tried to think about the meaning of my visit and about the decades I'd spent waiting for it, and I tried to decide—as though such decisions meant anything—which of the many places I'd lived in felt more real to me now that I'd finally seen Egypt again. I didn't know the answer. I thought of the lighter with my initials and of the Coca-Cola stand, of dark flannel trousers on warm sunny days, of Rome and of Linden Street, and of the girl in

whose studio this tale was born more than a quarter of a century
ago. I thought of Earl Grey tea, and of my tutors, and of the spoon
she had placed so deftly to my right before saying goodbye. I had
brought all these images with me, as if to free each one here, the
way ornithologists, having studied and labeled various birds in their
laboratories in North America, will travel all the way back to the
Amazon to release them in their natural habitat. I had come to
place each one like a tiny pebble at my grandfather's grave, already
sensing, as in "The Parable of the Talents," that I had perhaps been
a false steward for them, one "who has much received and renders
nothing back." I had stood and waited too long. Was this all I had to
show for the years? All I could think of were Wordsworth's own
words: *Was it for this?*

> Was it for this
> That one, the fairest of all rivers, loved
> To blend his murmurs with my nurse's song . . .

I did not want to answer the question. I did not want to be with
the dead. I suddenly wished I were elsewhere again.

When I had finished writing, that evening many years ago, and was
about to head home, I went over to the girl's kitchen sink to wash
my mug, but stopped short of doing so, depositing the mug in the
sink instead, after rinsing it somewhat, to show that I was civil but
not servile.

I remember, in the adjoining room, her bed undone. I remember the scent of her crumpled sheets when I leaned over and

touched them, as though they held deep secrets that I would never dare to ask about. And, as I surveyed her room, I thought to myself that it would take very little to persuade me to wait for her, especially since she had said I could, for I already knew not only that one day soon we would sleep together on this bed, between these very sheets, but that on the night when this did happen I'd look back on this moment when I stood up from the table, feeling quite pleased with myself and, stepping into her bedroom, swore to remember that, while thinking about Tintern Abbey and Alexandria and this girl and this bed and these sheets and everything else I wished to write about, I had also committed an act of arbitrage. I had marked this moment as one of those to which I knew I'd return many times over, and not just on our first night together but in future years as well, and in other homes, perhaps with other women, and in other cities, or in Alexandria itself, who knows, because it was not even this moment, or this place, or this girl that mattered anymore but how I'd woven my desire to live and be happy with each, and that even if nothing were to happen in my life to make me happy, the very act of thinking back on things could, in the end, make me no less happy than an experienced Ulysses waking up in Ithaca still thinking of the journey home.

Counterintuition

❊

On the inside of the back cover of my small Liddell and Scott *Greek-English Lexicon*, published by Oxford University Press and with me since my undergraduate days, is an address on MacDougal Street. It was written down in haste on May 27, 1969. Next to it is a telephone number. For weeks, eager to persuade myself that I was not so interested in the girl who had given it to me, I had refused to learn the number by heart. Nor had I yet called her often enough to commit it to memory, since the two of us were just barely starting what I failed to realize had already ended.

I began to feel things might have taken a wrong turn at Caffè Reggio on MacDougal Street on that hot June afternoon when, after I had waited about two hours, it began to dawn on me that this awful thing, which I'd vaguely heard someone call being stood up, had—unless I was totally mistaken—very possibly befallen me as well, and that the only way to prevent it from happening at all was for me to leave instantly, i.e., before it had definitely occurred.

The girl never apologized or made excuses. She didn't call, nor did she return my calls. I never forgave her and, probably, have made every woman pay for it since.

But because I had left Caffè Reggio in a flustered state on that hot afternoon in June, I began to suspect that perhaps she might have shown up after all, though very late, and that I owed her a call to determine whether it wasn't she, but I, who had to apologize.

To my college friends who assured me this was the most sublime piece of self-deception mounted by a spurned lover, I answered by saying I'd have agreed with them about any other girl, but that in this case things were just different. It did not occur to me that if there is one thing that makes all love stories identical, it's the conviction that each one is different.

But there was unfinished business at Caffè Reggio, and I would return that summer, sometimes more than once a day, the way not only criminals but victims, too, go back to the scene that made them who they are, seeking to recover something I felt I'd lost there, trying to become so familiar, so immune to Caffè Reggio as never to experience that disquieting ache each time I caught its name written by her hand on the back of my Liddell and Scott *Greek-English Lexicon*. I wanted to make the place mine, reinvent it, wash it down the way we wash down poison, blot it out, since I couldn't blot out the girl who had brought me to it. I wanted to steal Caffè Reggio from her, to banish her from it, and give it back only if she begged. I wanted to push back time, undo the memory of that afternoon and of the next one when I returned hoping I'd gotten the date wrong and of all the following ones when I came back thinking to retrieve what I'd lost when I walked out in a fury, saying, "That's it, I've waited long enough!" In the end, I wanted Caffè Reggio to remind me not of her but of me, the way I hoped she'd think of me and no one else when she'd eventually return.

Being at Caffè Reggio consisted in having to sit, smoke, and read, striking up an air of indifference that I felt would not only make me look attractive in case she did walk in but, by dint of being rehearsed every day, might persuade me that I'd ultimately grown indifferent and was well on my way to recovery.

I had learned this in one of the books I was reading that summer, *The Red and the Black*. If you like someone, brace yourself, don't show it; behave counterintuitively, keep zigzagging, feel with a forked heart, because such is the way of the world. If anything, show that you don't care, be distant. It will make her wonder, and in wondering she will warm to you, and in warming be snared. The formula was supposed to work. Never mind that the one person for whom it failed with abysmal regularity was the very author of *The Red and the Black*.

She called a year later. Did I want to go out that evening? Of course I did. By then I knew that if she'd called me it was only because I was the last in a long list. We went to see a movie. Then she had to run home.

Of course, my desperate phone calls amounted to nothing. Her mother, who took dutiful messages, always sided with me—surely an excellent sign, I thought, not realizing that mothers who side with spurned lovers are no more inclined to make things better for them than are their daughters. To forgive the daughter, I learned to hate the mother.

Another year passes. Then another. One weekday evening, same thing· she calls—would I like to go out? of course I would. We end up in the Village, on MacDougal Street, her favorite café, she says, forgetting she'd already told me all about her favorite café years earlier, while I'm feeling rather pleased with myself for resisting the needling impulse to say something either about the date-that-never-was or about this place, which is so layered with my own passage that it almost feels she's offered to come visit me at home.

And here we are, sitting in the back of Caffè Reggio, on my familiar little bench that feels more like a pew, and the place is crowded, everyone seems happy this weekday night in spring, and right by the large antique cylindrical espresso machine, she says, "Look at me," and begins kissing me. I wanted to tell her that this was precisely what I'd always dreamed of, that I'd almost given up, that I didn't know how I would ever come back here and go on as before after tonight. But I didn't interrupt.

Later, as we're walking up MacDougal and Washington Square, I look at her face and catch her smiling. Why is she smiling all the time? I ask. It dawns on me only then that I've been smiling all along, too. She leans against a wall and says, "Kiss me again." I thought she was testing herself, then I thought she was testing me, then I thought she was testing someone else she wanted to be with but wasn't. Or was it just me she wanted to be kissed by? I took her home. Her mother was sleeping in the adjacent room. After a while she said, hesitantly, that maybe I'd have to think of leaving. I did not press the point.

That night at home I sat at my desk sensing I had come full circle and was almost vindicated. From the young boy who'd been stood up on MacDougal Street I had become a man whose late-night advances had been uneasily staved off. I decided to jot down every single time I'd seen her, from the first on a subway platform, when I didn't know her name, to the time my heart had literally skipped a beat when I caught her standing right next to me at the library, to the moment this same evening when she walked me to her door on Fort Washington Road.

It never occurred to me that perhaps what she'd meant by her maybe I'd have to think of leaving was that I should stay awhile longer all the same.

I didn't see her again for another two years. By then I had

already graduated from college and was working. When we bumped into each other one day, I was almost indifferent, glad to be indifferent, eager to show that I was. It cost me almost nothing to say, "I was madly in love with you once." I made certain she knew I was speaking in postmortem terms. But I was, it occurred to me, trying too hard for someone who had given up trying. We even made light of our first kiss on the night of miracles. We made light of the people who had watched us from the other tables. We made light of her mother sleeping in the room next to the kitchen. "I live alone now," she said as we strolled toward Thompson Street afterward. Walking her to the door of her building, I hesitated a moment, then, without knowing what else to say, said goodbye, almost abruptly. "I thought you'd come upstairs," I heard her say. I went upstairs, almost reluctantly.

Until today, what I remember of the few weeks we spent together in the late spring of 1974 is the sight of MacDougal Street every morning, the smell of cigarettes and roasted coffee beans hovering on the sidewalks.

Three weeks later we argued.

A week after that, a friend wrote me a prescription for Valium. I showed her the prescription. Was that supposed to move her? she asked. Instead, she moved in with someone else.

The landlord, an Italian, had taken a liking to me. Did I want to assume her lease for the next six months? I said I would. One day, by common agreement, I walked out of the studio for a few hours. When I returned, everything that was hers was gone.

As I stood looking for the farewell note I knew it wasn't in her style to write, I vowed never to fall in love in quite that way again, and certainly never with a woman I couldn't understand, with whom the opposite of what I thought was always right except when I was sure I was wrong.

The number on the back of the Liddell and Scott *Greek-English Lexicon* means nothing to me now, but on it is inscribed a bizarre ache in the history of pain. The love may be gone—but the pain is hardly gone at all. I find it on the pavements of MacDougal Street on hot, steamy, midsummer afternoons, when the heat is unbearable, when, no matter how often they sprinkle the street or scour the sidewalks, something like a long, sleek blemish won't wash off. It never goes away, never went away, and stands there like one of those moments that cut us in two with a before and an after that stare at each other uncomprehendingly, like two strangers on opposite sidewalks, each looking away when their eyes meet, never for a second realizing that what stands between them is not just a missed opportunity but a possibility that never went away. It is still there and beckons still.

So here I stand a quarter of a century later.

It is a weekday, a late-December afternoon past four-thirty, and I'm on the corner of MacDougal and Bleecker Streets on my way to the Peacock Caffè a few blocks north. The day is just beginning to darken, and, after heavy showers this afternoon, everything glistens, the streetlights especially, speckling the wet pavement from one end of MacDougal to the other. I am, as happens so seldom, far ahead of time, enjoying this slow, damp, dreamy walk to Greenwich Avenue.

I like four-thirty. People are just beginning to come out of work, and there's a touch of indecision in the city, as though it's too late to start anything new today and yet still early enough to take a stab at it. Like me, most people are strolling about the streets, taking their time, probably avoiding something they should be doing, caught as everyone is in this interim dreamspace which is neither day nor night, hardly cold enough to prevent an extended walk, and yet almost cold enough for me to look forward to that warm drink in about an hour at the Peacock with my wife. It is, in short, and as anyone who's read Baudelaire knows, dusk. This is the time of day when those with busy night lives haven't yet picked out their clothes, while those at work, with loosened neckties and collars undone, can't wait to get out of theirs. It is the hour of the dressing room, when actors are not quite off the street but hardly yet onstage.

If I were an Elizabethan playwright, I'd seize on this very moment and call it an island, not off the coast of Naples, but an island in time, where one or more shipwrecked travelers are suddenly cast ashore on MacDougal Street and, with spellbound, startled eyes, find themselves suspended for a while at four-thirty between a falafel stand and a pastry shop, between MacDougal as it looks now and as it looked in the very late sixties.

I am also reminded of the fifty-two-year-old Stendhal sitting exhausted one warm day in September 1835 on a tiny bench along a solitary pathway by Lake Albano near Rome. Without knowing it, perhaps, he had picked the spot quite appropriately, for it is located right behind one of the stations of Calvary. Here Henri Beyle, a.k.a. Stendhal, a.k.a Dominique, a.k.a. Henri Brulard, a.k.a. so many other pseudonyms, will begin to contemplate the stations of his life. How does one of the most unfortunate lovers in French literature begin piecing together the fragments of his existence? How can someone who has had so much trouble connecting with others connect with his own life? What kind of narrative will he find? Is there a narrative?

One by one, Stendhal begins to scratch in the sand, in short-hand, the names of the women he has loved. This is how he charts, how he connects, the stations of his life, a life lived or rather told under the sign of Venus—even though, in his own words, "with all of these [women], as with others, I've always been a child; and I've had very little success." The abbreviated names are V, An, Ad, M, Mi, Al, Aine, Apg, Mde, C, G, Aur, and finally Mme Azur. These are the initials of the women he's loved. And yet, characteristically enough, next to Mme Azur he writes, "whose first name I forget." Another, Angela Pietragrua, is mentioned twice (once as An and once as Apg), because the two of them had resumed an affair after a hiatus of a few years.

"In fact," Stendhal writes, "I've possessed only six of the women I've loved." *Dans le fait, je n'ai eu que six de ces femmes que j'ai aimées.*

I was twenty-one when I first read *The Life of Henri Brulard,* and what baffled me most in Stendhal's list was its sheer length. Stendhal had loved and suffered for twelve women. I had scarcely loved one. I was intimidated, envious, dwarfed. It would never have occurred to me that thirty years later I'd be standing on Mac-Dougal Street trying to sort out the meaning behind my own list of initials, envying the young man who had envied the loves I've known.

I've stopped outside Caffè Reggio and am looking through the large glass panel. The place hasn't changed at all: dark, intention-ally faded interior, the old brown nineteenth-century furniture that seems lifted from yard sales in Naples and Palermo, the rounded green awning with the inscription *Since 1927,* the two large glass panels, the tiny one in between, and the little alcove in the back, which presumably must have housed a vintage telephone booth in the old days, and the glass door which opens with an intrusive squeak that makes everyone turn and stare forbiddingly, as I wonder whether I'll ever overcome this sense of being mildly unwelcome, of never really being "in" enough or bold enough or old enough to enter this tiny enclave of the happy few—jet-setter, movie-star types dressed in perpetual black, everyone so visibly and yet so unself-consciously, so transcendentally sexual, as though, when it came to these things, it is always I, and not another soul, who has the overly attentive, dirty mind. That much has never changed.

I don't know why I'm standing outside here, nor can I understand the words I keep saying to myself: *Nothing has changed. Nothing has changed.* This could easily be 1969, or 1975, or 1981.

I am feeling very awkward, as would a boy screwing up the courage to buy a pack of cigarettes, or a jealous man spying on his beloved. A man from a nearby falafel place has come out and is watching me. The waiter at Caffè Reggio catches me staring and assumes an inquisitive gaze. I was here many waiters ago, I want to boast, but it's nothing to boast about. A man sitting at a table by the window lifts his face and from behind the large pane clearly suggests I'm intruding on his space. I affect the focused expression of a subway passenger who's trying to look over and behind someone sitting in front of the map. Have I found what I'm looking for? he seems to ask. What I'm looking for has no name, I want to say, for it's like seeking a dead person—me, younger—at a cocktail party.

I am, of course, staring at the very last table in the corner, the one cast in a still darker shade of brown. But nothing comes: no revelation, no éclat. Should I, like a high-school student, like Stendhal in the sand, take out a penknife and carve into its old brown surface the coded names of the women I've loved?

With each new love, we invent a new way of charting our lives, of realigning our internal calendars. But where one sorrow should bury another, two sorrows coexist instead, face-to-face, like the young queen and the old queen sitting across the dinner table, each wishing the venom in her eyes were in the other's food—except that the two are in me, and the poison I take, I make.

This is Stendhal's narrative: at the time he knew A, he had no idea he'd meet B, or that C would devastate his life so thoroughly as to eclipse both A and B. And yet, despite everything, there was D waiting around the corner, D who would truly destroy him and before whom his suffering for C would pale into a trivial skit, so that a few years later, when he did run into C, all he could think was *When I lost her and thought life had ended, life hadn't even started. How can this be?* But as it turned out, this brief interlude with C, which was to salve an unhealed wound, proved worse than any injury inflicted by D, and one evening, totally distraught, he found himself knocking at D's door to forget C.

It would take nothing really for me to open the door to Caffè Reggio, where I haven't been in at least two years, and step into this island in time, into this bubble. If I'm hesitating it's not because I'm afraid of slipping into one of the many four-thirties I've known on this sidewalk but because I don't have the least inkling of whether it is an old fantasy I am tempted to revisit, a new fantasy, a memory, or an intricate cluster of unexpiated desires hovering not just over all the coffeehouses I've known in this neighborhood but over the evenings I've passed by, the films I've seen, the women I've fallen in and out of love with, down to those I never dared speak to but whose spirit all the same is forever present on the glistening pavements of MacDougal Street.

One of them lived a few blocks from here. For a few months we

came to Caffè Reggio every evening. Then she moved to another
city, and her table became my table, and I sat there with others,
until I, too, moved to another city, and someone else came in my
place, and someone after that, and so on, until I came back years
later and might as well have been as much a stranger to the last in a
generation of lovers as Odysseus returning to Ithaca.

I stare at the place now. What do I really want from it? Whom
am I hoping to find here? Or am I afraid of walking in and finding,
as in Fellini's 8½, or Eric Rohmer's *Chloe in the Afternoon*, Caffè
Reggio filled with all the women I've known, gathered in what
would of course be the ultimate surprise party from hell?

Or am I afraid of walking in and finding that I care for all of
them, that one never really unloves anyone in life but finds others
to love instead? Or, worse yet, that I've never cared for any and that
if I come here it's because I'm still lured by that vague, beguiling air
of possibility which continues to linger for me each time I come to
the Village.

Or am I afraid of finding Caffè Reggio totally empty but for one
table, occupied by one person, sitting as I had pictured her sitting
exactly thirty years ago to remind me that I've never forgotten her,
that she, too, may have never forgotten me, and that if I eventually
managed to forget her and have long ceased to love her, she
remains, to use Nietzsche's words, the "star love" of my life, the
quasar that lost its light but continues to exert silent gravitational
pull on every planet I've encountered?

Or is there another reason behind my fear: which is to walk into
Caffè Reggio and find that, despite the years and my attempts to
crowd them with people, the room is totally empty, because that,
too, is how it feels when I look back, seeing that, for someone
enamored of the past, I've never, ever kept in touch with the past

but have let it drift almost as though it weren't my past, because what was mine, ultimately, was not others but my dreams and fictions of others, which is to say, that what truly mattered was not their love but mine, mine despite theirs, me without them, the lonely me, the me that never goes away, the me who has no shape, no voice, no age, but who remains forever a wanting, angry, beseeching me, because I can never think of me except through others and am therefore always attached to something else, someone else, which is why I'm never in one spot, never in one person, never on one page or on one side of the street or one side of the table, but scattered in time as well, the way my West Village and Caffè Reggio is made up of scattered dates and scattered faces, where love, this would-be beacon punctuating the course of most lives because it subsumes so much hope for a better life, is itself nothing more than a trajectory without direction or purpose.

I decide to walk in.

I sit at the old familiar place. I order Earl Grey tea. I take out a sheet of paper. I draw up a list of names. I list the films I remember seeing near here or the number of times I've come here with someone and ordered Earl Grey tea. I play with numbers, with dates, trying to discern a pattern. I might as well have been making a list of stops on the Broadway Local.

Faced with the "bizarreness"—his word—of his life with women, Stendhal, who was as interested in tactical seduction as he was in romantic bliss, had come up with some kind of ideological compromise: if you love someone, you will find it very difficult to speak your heart; but speak from the heart you must. If you cannot speak, behave candidly, frankly, and naturally—and so long as you do this, you may succeed. Stendhal, an ex-mathematician, was also shrewd enough to catch the unstated term here: willed sincerity is just another mode of seduction, perhaps the most cunning mode of all. If, therefore, you are to be truly sincere, you must do the opposite of what you think you should be doing. That is, if you love someone, be cold. *Froid* is one of Stendhal's busiest adjectives. As Thomas Mann once said: The emotions are best served chilled. Nothing could have served Stendhal worse. Ultimately, we are as disingenuous with ourselves as we think others are with us.

And yet, even though I'm not an Elizabethan, and not a nineteenth-century man, this disingenuousness, this counterintuitiveness, speaks to my experience of life and of love just as it does to my experience of literature.

Toward the very end of 1974, I am working late one night when someone buzzes downstairs. I ask who it is. *"C'est moi,"* I hear someone say. I can't for the life of me place the voice, though it's not altogether unfamiliar: someone who speaks French and clearly knows me but whose familiar voice I can't place at all. It doesn't make sense. Without even thinking, I immediately discount the very first person who crosses my mind. She didn't know a word of French. Besides, since I've often caught myself thinking I'm hearing her voice, hoping it is her voice when I know it can't possibly be hers, I've trained my mind—counterintuitively—to spot itself playing tricks on me. I ask again. Through the static the exasperated voice finally blurts out: "Me, I said."

It's only after thinking a second that I begin to suspect it might actually be her; but the thought seems to be coming the long way around and from so very far away, like a plane that lands in some abandoned airfield in far-off Australia after many refueling stops along the way in Europe and Far East Asia on a long journey back to America. But this can't be. Only then did I grasp—

counterintuitively again—why I'd failed to recognize it; the voice wasn't really speaking French; it was merely imitating someone speaking French. She was—it took me a few seconds to realize—imitating *me*, assaulting me with exaggerated familiarity because she was a very shy person, concealing her shyness with the sassy fellowship of those who would otherwise overload their sentences with too many "maybe"s and "though"s. It was this sense of her shyness that finally suggested it could have been only one person and no one else.

A woman steps out of the old elevator. Had I merely been pretending it wasn't her so as not to be disappointed? Or—more counterintuitively yet—was I pretending it couldn't be her only to heighten the surprise, the pleasure, the miracle?

Her very long black hair is matted on her face; she's all wet, and I can't tell whether she's been crying or whether it's just the rain on her face. "Come in." I give her a bathrobe. She undresses in front of me. Then she goes to the linen closet and removes a large towel to dry her hair. In her place, I'd have pretended to forget where anything was after six months. Was this a good sign: I've come back, let's start all over again, I haven't forgotten anything? Or—counterintuitively (and I won't use the word any longer)—was this a bad sign: Don't go getting any ideas, I've got other worries on my mind?

I take her wet clothes, open the heat vent and hang them, light the stove, make tea. She's all white, shivers, sits on a chair, and gulps down the tea in hasty sobs. "He's thrown me out, you know." I rub her feet with alcohol and put wool socks on her feet. You'll sleep here tonight, we'll talk in the morning, I say. "He's thrown me out, you know," she repeats. Revenge is never kind, I think. This is the woman I would have done anything to kill. Now I'd do anything to kill the man who's thrown her back to me.

Still, I try to nudge the talk my way, to days when I'd look for the slightest pretext to skulk by their window each evening, finally getting caught by the very man who had given her back to me now. "But would you have stood outside his window the way I did?" I start to ask.

She instantly shoots me that old, embittered stare: "Why else do you think I'm soaked?"

She talks until very late. At one point I ask if she wants some brandy. She says she wants Valium instead. Do I still have those pills I'd taken because of her?

I do. How many does she want? The whole bottle, she says with a smile. I'd give it to her, except that I want one myself tonight.

When it's time to go to bed she says, "I don't want to sleep alone."

She came to me to forget him, she says, just as the pills I had taken to survive her loss would now help her survive my rival's.

Two days later she brought her things and moved in, the way I'd moved in with her. At night, when she slept, she'd mutter his name, or sometimes start with his, ending with mine.

Weeks later, she eventually managed to run into him, slept with him, said—hoping to please or appease me—that she had called him by my name at night.

I feigned exaggerated jealousy, perhaps to conceal that I was jealous indeed. Let's end it right now, I said. She did not argue.

Now I must go to him to forget you, she said, almost sheepishly, seeing the irony and making light of it, which is how she suffered. We made up. Besides, I would soon be moving to Boston. Did I still want the apartment? No, she could have it back.

I remember our last evenings in a crowded Caffè Reggio in the winter of 1974 and how sad we both were, neither in love with the other and yet thrown together like opposites who've finally understood that opposites seldom attract. She had lost the man she loved. And I, too, had just lost a girl I'd met earlier that same summer. We would speak about both, at once pleased that we could and yet piqued that each had someone else, each finding that a heart can ache in two places at the same time and still spit venom and its antidote without skipping a beat. She desperately wanted him to catch us at the back corner table, and I desperately wanted to be seen by my old flame. It brought us together, and as we walked up and down Thompson and Sullivan, I'd force an arm around her hips, and she yielded, thinking, perhaps, If he wants to so badly, then let him, mistaking it for passion, not knowing that I'd already second-guessed her kisses to be no different from my own. They were third-party kisses; we kissed as we loved, with our eyes open, the counterfeit and its replica locked in a mock embrace which, perhaps, still counted for something.

We said goodbye near Washington Square, promising to write or call. But I never heard from her again. The last time I saw her handwriting was on an envelope she had forwarded to my address in Boston. It was a letter from my previous girlfriend asking why I'd disconnected my phone.

There must be a meaning to this pattern, but I don't know its name.

One night in the sixties I caught sight of a beautiful girl in the library who looked quite familiar. When our eyes met again, she smiled, I smiled back, and, without thinking, finally mustered the courage to speak. I know you from somewhere. Yes, you look familiar, too. We dropped a few names: friends, places, teachers, courses, parties. No, no one in common, nothing in common, totally different tastes. It was only as we were talking that I began to realize—and from the look in her eyes it seemed she sensed it before I did—that we knew each other from having stared at each other one day on a subway platform and again a few days later, and again that very morning, and that if, in speaking to her, I had now crossed a line my own shyness should never have allowed me to cross, it was only by mistake, which is how I always asked for the things I wanted in life, whereas she, by thinking I'd had the gumption to pretend I'd forgotten where we'd seen each other before, had, by another twisted process, made a corresponding mistake. Had I figured all this out before opening my mouth, my life would have taken an entirely different turn. I wouldn't have spoken to her, wouldn't have known so much heartache, wouldn't have learned to read life inside out, wouldn't have lived it as though it were a downhill slalom studded with buried obstructions and perilous counterturns.

All this, and more, is still inscribed in the telephone number in the back of my *Greek-English Lexicon*. When I said to her, "Then let me have your number," as though it were the most casual request in the world, the way she volunteered to write it down seemed so amused, so serene, and so propitious that even today it is difficult to read in the royal blue of her handwriting a hint of what was awaiting me at MacDougal and Bleecker.

Which is where I'm standing now. An hour has passed since I walked into Caffè Reggio. Against the glistening reflection of the streetlights and other signs of an evening already wearing into night, a setting sun has just broken through the clouds to cast a hazy orange glow—the last few minutes of an afternoon that almost never was. Dusk has barely even started, the day—as people leaving a matinee are always pleased to find—is still young, dinner with the person I love most is still hours away, and this tale I have remembered after so many years has, once again, been put behind me.

And yet, as I hurry on my way to the Peacock, I am grateful beyond words that I can remember, grateful even to known that, despite the far better things life has given me many years since, the one moment I'll never be able to live down is when a girl, whispering from across a narrow table in her mother's kitchen, offered me a blank check to life that I, almost without thinking, turned into a rain check. Perhaps I would do no differently today. And therein lies both comfort and sorrow. To measure time by how little we change is to find how little we've lived; but to measure time by how much we've lost is to wish we hadn't changed at all. There are ledgers that stay open all life, there are scores we'll never repay. And to stare at these is to wander onto Prospero's island, where strange spirits speak with a forked tongue when they aren't lying to us, but where each truth about ourselves is a tongue-twister meant to trounce everything we know. For the tempest is not just what brings us to the island. The tempest is the island. It is the insoluble knot we can't leave behind but bring with us wherever we go, it is who we are when we are alone and no one else is looking, please: it is how we tussle with the one person we can never outgrow but fear we'll never become. It is, in the end, how we make sense of our lives when we know there is no sense to be made.